ME, MYSELF & YOU

Also by Vincent P. Collins

Acceptance
Grief
Partnership

ME, MYSELF & YOU

Revised Edition

By Vincent P. Collins

Abbey Press
St. Meinrad, IN 47577

To Austin B. Ripley

First published 1969
Revised and enlarged edition September 1974
Second printing November 1974
Third printing March 1975
Fourth printing October 1975
Fifth printing March 1976
Sixth printing June 1977
Seventh printing August 1978
Eighth printing November 1978
Ninth printing March 1980
Tenth printing January 1981

Library of Congress Catalog Card Number: 74-17734
ISBN: 0-87029-001-0
Printed in the United States of America

Abbey Press
St. Meinrad, Indiana 47577

Contents

FOREWORD

This booklet was written to enable people to live in such a way as to be happier with themselves, their situation, and other people. It embodies the "Live and Let Live" philosophy of life. If it boasted a subtitle, it might well be "HOW NOT TO LET PEOPLE BUG YOU." There is nothing theoretical about it—it is designed for action. It answers the question "What?" rather than "Why?" It is practical in the same sense that a good cookbook is practical: all the recipes have been kitchen-tested time and time again. They are effective if you follow them exactly.

Anyone can understand and use the "Live and Let Live" philosophy without formal training in psychology. It is a pragmatic, non-theoretical but comprehensive and effective way of meeting and solving the emotional problems attendant on our fast-paced modern living.

Undoubtedly, every age has been an age of stress. Ours is no exception. Stress and tension daily make more and more of us uncomfortable, even to the point of nervous exhaustion. So many of us have mental and emotional problems that there are just not enough psychotherapists to go around. What is needed is a simple and effective therapy which can be administered by the individual himself, or by any one in a counselling situation—the doctor, visiting nurse, caseworker, clergyman, or teacher. Hopefully, this book will fill the need.

—*Vincent P. Collins*

Foreword to Revised Edition

ME, MYSELF and YOU was written "to enable people to live in such a way as to be happier with themselves, their situation, and other people." Since the time of publication, I have learned more helpful hints for more comfortable living from people who read the first edition, and I have incorporated them in this revision.

One of the most consistent reactions of readers has been: "Why didn't you say more about the place God should play in life?" I told them honestly that I didn't want to be considered a Holy Joe or a religious fanatic; and that I hated to consider God as a "therapeutic agent". In other words, to *use* God. Whereat I was told rather tartly that they thought God wouldn't really mind. I came back with: "But it might turn people off." So they merely quoted me to me: "If so, that's *their* problem."

You will find a new section in the book entitled "Me and God." I make no apologies for it—after all, emotional maturity is the complete acceptance of reality. He is the Supreme Reality.

—*Vincent P. Collins*
June, 1974

PART I

ME VS. MYSELF

THE DAISIES

You might say that daisies have it made. No problems, no troubles, no hang-ups, no heartaches. No work, all play. Nothing to do but look pretty and enjoy the sunshine. Get along just fine with themselves and other daisies. For them, "the living is easy;" just a matter of growing, reproducing and fading away, "just doing what comes naturally." Nothing bugs them, not even bugs. Their little world of sun, air, earth and water does not include pain, suffering, trouble, fear, frustration, or any of those things that are found in the world of human beings. Their world suits them fine. Never crosses them or lets them down. Yessir, daisies have it made!

Ever wish you were a daisy? If so, one couldn't really blame you. Everyone has times when he envies the daisies. When life gets to be too much of a struggle, when you feel as if you were up to your neck in a swift stream, fighting against the current, swimming with might and main and not even keeping even, —that's when you come to envy the plants and animals. That's when you are tempted to ask, "Is living worth the struggle?" If that is the way you sometimes feel, this booklet may be of some help to you.

THE SCHOOL OF LIFE

Life is no picnic. No sense in denying it. It involves problems, troubles and heartaches. Problems with yourself, with the world around you. It has always been that way. Living involves a struggle for food, clothing, and shelter. The struggle for mastery of yourself. The struggle with others for your rights. The struggle to fulfill needs the daisy never heard of: the need to love and be loved; to be respected as an individual; spiritual needs and emotional needs. Unlike the daisy, you and I have needs that Nature cannot fill.

To live as a human being or, more to the point, to live happily as a human being requires much more than "just doing what comes naturally." It has to be learned. You weren't born with the knowledge that you need in order to do a successful job of living. Nature did not equip you with the technique of providing yourself food, clothing and shelter, to say nothing of the technique of living comfortably with yourself and others. Most people quickly learn how to provide for their physical needs, but all too many, through no fault of their own, go through life without learning how to provide for their emotional and spiritual needs. In short, they never learn "to live and let live." Hence this book whose aim is to outline the things that are essential to happy living and point out practical rules for accomplishing them.

Comfortable Living Takes Some Doing

HAPPY LIVING

One has to learn to like olives. This is known as a "learned phenomenon." Living in such a way as to be happy is also a "learned phenomenon." Getting happy and staying happy isn't a question of luck. It's not a hit or miss proposition. You don't get it from the ground. Living is a science and an art. It is a science in the sense that it embodies knowledge. It encompasses certain basic principles which must be taught, studied and learned. It is an art in the sense that it involves skill, that is, practice, as well as theory; doing as well as knowing. If your life is unhappy, the chances are that you never have been taught the principles, or, having learned them, decided that it was too much trouble to practice them. Or it may be that you did learn the theory and were putting it into practice when something knocked you for a loop and you lost the knack. At any rate, the fact remains that happy living can be learned and the art can be acquired if you are willing to learn what to do, roll up your sleeves, make with the muscles, and get at it. Some of the things you will be advised to do may be just the opposite of what you have been doing, but what have you got to lose? It's worth a try!

There are three major obstacles to happy living. They are, in order of importance: injurious feelings, overreaction to others, and confusion as to your place in the scheme of things. We will examine these in detail and discuss practical ways of meeting them. The basic principle is simple enough. You ascertain just what is subject to your control and what is beyond your control. Then you learn how to control what can be controlled, inside and outside yourself, and how to come to terms with persons and circumstances that are beyond your control. The key word is "control." Control of your feelings, thoughts and impulses. Control of your demands on yourself.

Learn How to Control
Everything That Is Subject
to Your Control
Forget About What's
Beyond Your Control

DO HAVE A BREAKDOWN!

Not an easy job, learning to live. A big order, indeed. But not really too big, for it is being done by thousands and thousands of ordinary, average people like yourself. A fortunate few were born with a natural knack for living, but most of us poor souls have had to learn the hard way. One of the hard ways is the breakdown route. You get there by reaching a point in life where you feel you just can't cope, surrender to the fact, and holler for help. I wouldn't recommend it, but actually there's nothing like a good breakdown to get started on the track to comfortable living. Providing, that is, that you get the right help, that you become willing to give up some of your cherished beliefs and practices, do violence to your obstreperous feelings, and work at it. If you do, you get to find life at first tolerable, then comfortable, and finally downright enjoyable. But even if you have not (as yet?) had the advantage of having a breakdown, you may learn how to live comfortably with yourself and others, and even how to help others do the same. You can learn to live and let live.

A Breakdown Can
Make You Or Break You.
(Better It Should Make You!)

LIVE!

"LIVE!" What does that mean? It means different things to different people. It means whatever you want it to mean. To some, "to live" means "to live it up", that is, to crowd all the pleasure possible into a lifetime. To others, "to live" means to get as much as possible of the "Three P's"—Possession, Pleasure and Power (Status). To the ambitious, it means to succeed, that is, to make one's mark in politics, business or the arts—to become famous, well-known, or at least recognized as outstanding in one's profession. There are probably as many definitions of "living" as there are persons. What's yours? In my experience, the people who have really learned how to live are those who have learned to live comfortably with themselves and others. Generally, they have learned through suffering. Their secret, insofar as I can figure it out, seems to be that they have learned how to live their own lives and let others live theirs. In learning how to live, they have learned to let live, and in learning how to let live, they have learned to live. They respect themselves and they respect others. They have learned to control themselves without allowing others to control them and in the process they have learned not to attempt to control others. They have peace, serenity, contentment.

You Can Learn How to Live Comfortably with Yourself and Others

ONE DAY AT A TIME

Many have said it, but none more beautifully than Robert Louis Stevenson:

Anyone can carry his burden, however heavy, until nightfall. Anyone can do his work, however hard, for one day. Anyone can live sweetly, patiently, lovingly, purely, till the sun goes down. And that is all that life really means.

Live one day at a time! Plan for tomorrow, but live today. Never extend the range of your concern beyond bedtime tonight. Hold out till then. Plan for tomorrow, but don't worry about it. Time enough to worry about it when it comes. "Give us this day our daily bread." If you have an especially difficult problem, find out whether or not you can do anything about it today. If there is something you can do about it, do it—do it right now; don't put it off. It may be harder to do it now than to put it off, but you suffer less in the long run. If

there is nothing you can do about it today,
then resolve not to think about it again until
such time as you can do something about it.
Time enough to think about it then. Meanwhile, put it in God's hands, and try to forget
it.

Live One Day
At a Time

IT DOESN'T MATTER

Overreacting to trivial things seems to be a basic trait of human nature. What was it that got you so shook up just a week ago? I'll bet you can't remember. What was that earth-shaking tragedy of ten years ago that (you thought at the time) was going to ruin your life? Have to stop and think, don't you? Here's a secret: nothing in this life matters but life itself, its beginning and its end. Everything else is trivial. You have already been born; inevitably you will die. Birth and death are beyond your control. There is nothing you can do about them. You will survive until you die. Anything that does not affect your ability to keep breathing is trivial. Short of that, nothing really matters. All that really matters is to keep breathing; and only, by the way, to keep breathing until bedtime tonight!

Pick out the thing that bugs you most in your life. Every time it enters your mind, say: "It doesn't matter!" Of course, you don't really believe this. And, at first, every time you tell yourself that it doesn't matter, the bad little boy in your stomach will come right back: "Who you trying to kid?" Like heck it doesn't matter! But keep on, day after day, saying thousands of times whenever you begin to get shook up about anything: "It doesn't matter!" This is called "do-it-yourself brainwashing," and it works. It works fabulously. You can't do it enough. Don't be afraid that you will wind up like the mother who went to the psychiatrist and told him that her little boy was driving her crazy. He put her under heavy medication. When she returned a week later he said, "How are you making out with your little boy?" With a blank stare she answered, "What little boy?" This may be somewhat exaggerated, but it gets across the general idea. Try this for six weeks—saying "It doesn't matter" to anything and everything—and we'll guarantee that life will be much more liveable.

Nothing Matters
Except
To Keep Breathing

WHO'S "YOU"?

It was stated above that the first obstacle to comfortable living is your feelings; in other words, you. If you are going to live your own life, you'd better be darned certain sure that it is really you who are living it; that when you make a decision, it is really you who are making it. Those decisions that you think you are making are quite possibly not being made by you at all. You are probably not aware of it, but there is more than one "You." There is the real you, the "You" of the mind and will, and then there is the "Pseudo-You," the "You" of the feelings, the Emotional You. When we speak of your living your own life, it is of the real "You" we are speaking, the responsible, mature "You," not the pseudo-you, the immature you, the emotional you of your feelings.

You may be living your own life in the sense that no one outside of you is dictating what you must think or what you must do. That still does not mean that you are living your own life. There may well be someone in-side you who is imperiously dictating what you must think and what you must do. There is more than an outside chance that you cannot really "call your soul your own." Why? Because you may be at the mercy of an irrational, childish, immature "Other-self." Don't laugh! To call your soul your own, your thoughts and actions must be under the con-trol of your mind and will. They should never be governed by the feelings or emotions. Feelings have their place in your life, a very necessary place, but they are not supposed to run your life for you. They are to you what the motor is to the automobile. The motor sup-plies the power. It is not intended to take the place of the driver. Your emotions must never be allowed to take over the wheel. While the Real You can never completely overcome the influence of the Emotional You, you must never let him get in the driver's seat. Your will must retain its freedom of choice and action. If you allow your feelings to dictate your behavior, you have become a driverless automobile, careening down the highway of life, headed for a crackup.

Control Your Feelings, or They Will Control You

THE ENEMY WITHIN

Know your enemy! You may think that every threat to your peace of mind comes from outside. Not so! The main threat to your happiness and serenity is more subtle, harder to pin down, to identify and to control than any influence that can be brought to bear on you from the outside. That threat is an unsuspected, sabotaging fifth columnist who is right inside you. You may be completely unaware of his existence. Now is the time to identify him and smoke him out.

Deep down in the core of your being (perhaps in the vicinity of your stomach) there lives a scared, mean, spiteful, vicious little boy (or girl, as the case may be) who reacts to every situation with fear or resentment, panic or rage. He has been hiding out there since you were born. You grew up, but he never did. He's still three years old. We'll call him "Buster" (if you're a "he"; "Brat," if you're a "she"). He is very easily frightened, angered, or worried. Many times when you experience fear, anger, or worry, you believe that it is you who are afraid, angered, or worried. It isn't you at all; it's Buster. He has done a pretty good job of convincing you that he is you. He is not the real you. He is the immature, self-centered, suspicious, resentful, even desperate three-year-old "you." Buster must be disciplined, trained, brought into line. For his own good, you must stop coddling him. He must be forced into growing up. He is your enemy now, but you can make him your staunchest ally. He can contribute as much to your future happiness as he has to your past and present misery. Like any bewildered child, he doesn't really want to run things and does so only by default. Meanwhile, he does the best he can—a pretty poor best.

Know
The Real "You"

THREE-YEAR-OLDS

Note that I am not asking you to argue with your feelings; I am suggesting that you take action. You can no more win an argument with Buster than you can with any other three-year-old. You know how it goes: "Mommie, I want a cookie." "No, not now—I'm busy getting dinner." "Why can't I have a cookie?" "Because it's too near dinner time! It'll spoil your dinner." Then five minutes later, "All right, here's a cookie; now get out of here!" The only successful way to win an argument of this kind is not to argue. "No, you can't have a cookie; never mind why. Now git!" This holds true also of that three-year-old who lives in your tummy: "Stop it right this minute!"

Never Try To Reason
With Feelings
-Command Them!

SPOT THE VILLAIN

Before you can take measures to overcome an enemy, you must know who he is, and what he's up to. As we have seen, our enemy is a fifth columnist and saboteur; he is right inside the walls. You must be constantly on guard against his operations, and the minute he shows his head, whack it. Your enemy is the spoiled little brat who is trying to take you over. It is easy to spot his activity; he gives himself away by feelings of anger, resentment, envy, fear, anxiety, unwarranted guilt or self-pity. The minute you spot any of these poisonous feelings rising up deep in your being, squelch them: "STOP IT!" Don't make the mistake of accepting his suggestions and working them up in your mind, strengthening them—the more you think about them the stronger they get, and the stronger they get the more you think about them. Ignore them, banish them as soon as they are spotted, and deliberately turn your mind to some other train of thought.

Spot It
And
Stop It!

DISCOURAGEMENT

It has taken a lifetime for you to build up the habit of giving in to your feelings, and you won't be able to form new reaction patterns overnight. So you will have failures, relapses, setbacks. It is a matter of two steps forward, one step backward. When you have been making progress and doing well, there is always the danger that a setback will throw you. The setback is harmful only if you take it seriously: "I'm not any better, I'll never get any better, etc." It is harmless if you attach no importance to it; as FDR said at a critical moment in history: "The only thing we have to fear is fear itself." There will be setbacks—everyone has his bad days—but they are not significant; the significance that you may persist in attaching to them is the only significance they have. So ignore them. Get up from the canvas and get on with it.

Discouragement is, after all, just a feeling. It seldom has any basis in fact. You deal with it as you deal with any other feeling: ignore it, put it out of your mind, and think of something else. Above all, take action. Do something, if it's only taking a walk down the street. Make with the muscles! After all, you're no better than Abraham Lincoln.

"Every night," he said, "I make up my mind to resign." But he didn't. And neither should you.

Setbacks Are Part of Life. Don't Let Them Throw You

POOR BUSTER (BRAT)

Buster's main trouble is that he can't think, he can only feel. He has been passing his feelings on to you disguised as thoughts. Every time you dwell on thoughts of anger, resentment, envy, jealousy, anxiety, apprehension, self-doubt, inadequacy, self-pity, guilt and the like, be assured that Buster's at the bottom of it. In addition to serving feelings up as thoughts, he has another disagreeable talent that can contribute to your lack of ease. It is his imagination. Like all three-year olds, Buster has a very vivid and active imagination. It goes into action immediately, whenever his feelings are aroused. Like feelings, imagination is necessary to our human way of life. It is a great asset to be able to picture things in the mind's eye, but like feelings, it can be harmful when it gets out of line.

The imagination translates thoughts and feelings into mental pictures. If the thoughts and feelings are beneficial, so are the mental pictures. If the thoughts and feelings are harmful, so are the images. The imagination intensifies the thoughts and feelings. Suppose you begin to think of something you fear excessively—flying for instance. Buster's projector goes right into action, and whammo!—there it is before your mind's eye in wide-screen living color: the plane crashing with a bang right into a mountainside! To a "white-knuckle" airline patron, the thought of flying gives rise to the feeling of fear, and the imagination wastes no time in taking over. The process continues, each element intensifying the other until you panic. There is only one way to overcome it: break the buildup cycle. Squash the feeling. Banish the thought. Turn off the projector.

Buster may be called many things: the subliminal self, the immature self, the emotional self, the lower self, the pseudo-self. But whatever tag you may put on him, he's bad news. He's engaged in a struggle with you right this minute to determine who's going to be boss: he or you. You'd better decide that right now. Or has he already decided it for you?

Will the Real
"You"
Stand Up?

THE BUILDUP

As we just saw, the reaction process is further complicated by the faculty of the mind which we call "imagination." Imagination is to the emotions what illustrations are to a text, what music is to a ballad. It is the ability to form mental pictures, to visualize irritating or fearful situations in concrete form. As soon as we perceive a feeling and begin to think about it, the imagination goes to work. The imagination reinforces the thoughts, the thoughts intensify the feelings, and the whole business builds up. There is only one way to beat this game, and that is to stop the thoughts in their tracks and block out the imaginary pictures. Fearful or angry feelings and thoughts generate pressure, and the pressure will continue to increase as long as the buildup process is allowed to continue. We can't afford pressure. It's no good to "sit on the lid" after we have built up a good head of steam, and it's not much better to "blow off" steam. It is much better not to build up a head of steam in the first place.

Stop the Buildup
Before It Starts

SENSATIONS

There is another secret weapon that Buster has up his sleeve, in addition to disagreeable feelings and imaginings. It consists of unpleasant physical sensations, such as palpitations, tremors, pressures, aches and pains, nervous fatigue, and dizziness, to name a few. You probably never dreamed that Buster is at the bottom of them, accepting them at face value as symptoms of some physical disorder. Experience has taught you that you get these sensations after a bout with your feelings. Whenever you are emotionally upset, the sensations appear. So you begin to feel that it would be better to give in to the feelings and spare yourself the discomfort of the sensations. What you don't realize is that giving in to the feelings doesn't cure the sensations. As a matter of fact, the opposite is true. The way to overcome the sensations is to go ahead and do the thing you fear to do. This is the only way they can be mastered. Suppose you shake uncontrollably when you speak in public. You have to avoid invitations to speak for that reason. What you should do is to speak in public every chance you get, and ignore the shakes. Pretty soon there won't be any shakes. The reason for this is that while you are convinced that it is the public speaking you are afraid of, the thing you really fear is the sensations that are brought on by the thought of the public speaking. Once you realize this fact, accept it and begin to act on it. Once you've proved to yourself that it's the sensations and not the action that is at the root of the trouble, your troubles are over.

It's Not the Action Itself
That Causes You to be Afraid
It's the Distressing Sensations
Ignore the Sensations
And Perform the Action

NEUROTIC SYMPTOMS

Physical sensations induced by stress situations are distressing enough in themselves, but they can lead to an even more distressing phenomenon. They may lead you to believe that you have an illness when you actually have none. That is, you may have physical sensations which you mistake for symptoms of some serious illness. For instance, you take the palpitations that arise in a stress situation to be symptoms of a serious heart condition. A stomachache is interpreted as evidence of an ulcer. A headache betokens a brain tumor. And anything and everything is symptomatic of (shhhhhhh!) cancer.

If you are building your aches and pains into some dreadful pathological condition, wait a minute. Before you call up the friendly undertaker, get to your family physician and have a thorough physical examination. If there is something amiss, he will tell you about it and prescribe treatment. If he gives you a clean bill of health, for heaven's sake, please take his word for it! Place the blame for your imaginary ailment where it rightfully belongs: on Buster. Ignore all his little ploys, the pressures, aches, pains and what-all. Better yet, laugh at them and thank God that they are symptomatic of nervous strain rather than of physical disintegration.

Don't Take Symptoms Of Imaginary Ailments Seriously

EMOTIONS

Buster has a secret weakness. You can make one of his little stratagems work for you rather than against you. That panicky feeling that you get in your stomach when you suffer from a guilt feeling, for example, is the tip-off that the feeling you are experiencing has absolutely no basis in reality. Physical sensations are often indications of emotional mischief. They can help you to tell the difference between valid feelings and exaggerated emotional reactions. It works this way: if an anxious or guilty feeling is accompanied by a sensation such as, for example, "butterflies in the stomach," it is a good sign that your anxiety or guilt is unwarranted. This is invariably true of "that panicky feeling." You can make it work for you instead of against you. Whenever you notice that a guilty feeling is accompanied by a panicky feeling, be assured that the guilt you feel is nonexistent. It is a feeling, not a fact. Pay no attention to it. Say to yourself, "not guilty!" and forget it.

The whole matter of feelings, emotions, appetites and drives is highly complicated. If you are confused about it, don't let it bother you. Wiser men than we have become frustrated when they started to delve into this mysterious area of the human personality. Let's simplify it as much as possible by confining our inquiry to two basic personality functions: feeling and emotions. A feeling is an instinctive, unconscious, reflex physical reaction to a situation. An emotion is the feeling plus another element: self-awareness. That is to say, an emotion is a feeling of which we have become aware in our consciousness. The process goes something like this: we find ourself in a dangerous situation. We react to it instinctively, automatically, with a feeling of fright. Then we become conscious of the fact that we are frightened. Then we think about the feeling and about the situation which is causing it. The instinctive feeling has been intensified by the application of our conscious mind to it; the resultant combination of feeling and thought is called an "emotion." The feeling is a physical reaction; the emotion takes the feeling to the mental level, involving mind as well as body. It is not the initial feeling which causes us trouble, but the emotion which grows out of it.

Turn The Panicky Feeling From A Liability Into An Asset

NECESSARY EVIL

Not all feelings are bad or injurious; and even some of the "bad" feelings serve a useful purpose. They are essential to our self-preservation. Take fear, for instance. Suppose you were incapable of fear. In the middle of the street you see a huge truck bearing down upon you. You react thus: "My, this is interesting! I do believe that he is going to run me down. Wonder what will happen? Perhaps I should move." By that time it has already happened. In actuality, you see the truck and before you even stop to think, you make a flying leap for the curb—an instinctive reflex which saves your life. Your glandular system, from the hypothalamus down, is a complicated defense network which goes into action automatically. The sight of the truck triggers it and your feet do the rest. In the face of a real and present danger, fear is invaluable. It does have a drawback, however; it is blind. It gives the command, "Battle stations!" whenever it receives a message from your sense faculties. It never knows whether the danger to which it is alerted is real or imaginary, cold fact or fantasy, and it can't afford to take the time to decide.

The difficulty arises when the message to the defense network is inaccurate or exaggerated. Stress makes people worry where there is no cause to worry, to see danger where there is no danger. Continual apprehension keeps the network on battle alert constantly. Tension builds up tension, and the process snowballs. The glandular system reacts to the cry of "Danger!" with the command, "Clear the decks for action!" The muscles tense, the pulse accelerates, the adrenalin pours into the blood stream. The physical tension feeds back to increase the original feeling of fear, and the vicious cycle is set in motion. The fear is built up and built up until panic results. Repeat this process enough times, until it becomes habitual, and a breakdown is inevitable. A person just cannot continue to live with unremitting tension. The emotions are hard taskmasters. The engine is in the driver's seat and the driver becomes the unwilling passenger. He is being "taken for a ride." Some ride!

Feelings Aren't Facts
Because You Feel
A Thing Is So
Doesn't Make It so

DAISIES AND DOGGIES

Daisies, to get back to our introductory theme, have no feelings, no brains, and no problems. Doggies are different. Doggies have feelings, but very limited brains. Their consciousness is limited. This is lucky for them. They feel fear and act instinctively on the feeling: flight, if possible; fight, if cornered. That's all there is to it, for them. They are not subject to the building-up or working-up process. When a bigger dog comes snarling into the alley, Doggie feels fear, and takes to his heels immediately. He doesn't take time out to think about it. "Boy, was that close! Am I ever scared! What if he comes back?" Not at all; he doesn't give it a thought—he has no thoughts to give. He perceives, reacts, and that's the end of it. We could take a lesson from him. His feelings are an asset to him, not a liability. Do the thing, don't think about it. And when it's done, forget it!

The big difference between man and dog is that man can think about himself. He is conscious of himself as the subject of his feelings; he is conscious of what he is thinking and feeling, whereas the dog is not. Doggie just feels, period. Man intensifies his feelings simply by being conscious of them. We can take a little incident which irritates us and keep hashing it over and rehashing it until we work ourselves into a first class rage. We can take some minor inconvenience and work it up into a cause for murder. We can make a mountain out of a molehill just by thinking and thinking and thinking about it. "Conscience maketh cowards of us all." By the same token, thinking can drive us crazy.

Don't Work
Your Feelings Up
By Thinking About Them
Ignore Them and Let
Them Die Away

FEELINGS VS. FACTS

When is thinking not thinking? When it's feeling disguised as thinking. How many times do you say, "I think so and so," when what you really mean is, "I feel so and so"? You resent being told that you are merely voicing a feeling when you are convinced that you are rendering an opinion or judgment. This is mistaking feeling for thoughts, and you will never get to live comfortably with yourself until you stop the practice. Feelings aren't facts! Just because you feel that a thing is so doesn't necessarily make it so. For instance, you may feel that everyone in the world is in league against you, but that doesn't prove that such is the case. You may feel that you are no good to yourself or anyone else, and that everyone would be better off if you were dead, but again, that doesn't prove anything. You may refuse to drive an automobile because you have a feeling that you will kill somebody. You may feel that you just can't go into a supermarket or a church, or even use the phone, go beyond your block, or heavens knows how many other things. You may "feel" that if you try to do any of these things you'll "faint" dead away. If this is the way it is with you, Buster has surely done a good job on you, hasn't he? All of these judgments and convictions of yours aren't your thoughts. They're Buster's feelings. So defy him. Tell him to shut up and then go ahead and drive, phone, shop, go to church, or whatever else it is you feel you just can't do. The more often, the better. You won't faint dead away. You'll begin to feel better than you have in years.

Stop Taking
Your Feelings Seriously
And Acting On Them
As If They Were
Valid Judgments

POISON

Not all feelings are bad for us. There are feelings and feelings, beneficial feelings as well as injurious. We need beneficial feelings, such as satisfaction, accomplishment, hope, admiration, benevolence, love, affection, and a host of others. They are good for us, indeed, they are essential to happiness. The injurious feelings, such as anxiety, worry, fear, resentment, envy, anger, hate, self-doubt, self-disgust, inadequacy, self-pity and unwarranted guilt can do us a lot of harm. You don't need them. They are poison to the heart and mind. You can never afford the luxury of coddling them, dwelling on them, thinking about them, building them up. This is a rule which admits of no exceptions whatsoever. You can't afford to indulge anger, for instance, even when everyone will agree with you that you have every just reason in the world to be angry. Whether your anger is "justified" or not, you simply can't afford it. All reasons to the contrary notwithstanding, there is one overriding and decisive reason why you should not give in to anger: it's very bad for you. It does you harm. The same holds true for self-pity. You may have a list as long as your arm of reasons why you should feel sorry for yourself, but that makes no difference: you just cannot afford to feel sorry for yourself. Recognize harmful feelings for what they are: poison. Treat them as such!

You Just Can't Afford The Luxury of Anxiety, Worry, Fear, Resentment, Anger, Hate, Envy, Jealousy, Self-Pity, or Unwarranted Guilt

<u>DON'T</u> THINK!

You have probably seen the black-framed signs in large type saying THINK! all over the country. Well, they are the invention of a certain Mr. Watson, founder of IBM. Every time I see one I feel an almost irrepressible urge to cross it out with a black crayon or slash it with a pocket knife. What is good for IBM isn't necessarily good for the country. Thinking can be the worst thing in the world for you, if you have an unresolvable problem, an inescapable situation, an overmastering fear, or a crushing anxiety in the face of which you feel helpless. What do you do?—Put it out of your mind! If there is anything at all you can do about it here and now, do it this minute. If there isn't, put it out of your mind until such time as you can do something about it. Establish a deadline, like—say—three months from now. If you can do something today, do it today. Putting it off will just add to the pressure and make it harder in the end than it would be to do it and get it over with.

WHAT TO DO

Rampaging feelings present a real threat to our happiness and peace of mind. They pose a very serious problem. However, the problem is not insurmountable. It can be solved. The solution is anything but involved, complicated or mysterious. It is very simple. So simple that you probably will think it can't possibly be effective. It can work and it does work if you work at it. We know that feelings can't be controlled directly. They are blind; they can't be argued with, because they won't "listen to reason." Indirectly, however, you can control your feelings by controlling your thoughts. Thoughts can be controlled; they can be turned on and off at will, with practice.

How do you go about controlling your thoughts? You do it by a process of do-it-yourself brainwashing. Whenever you spot a fearful or angry thought, you repeat to yourself over and over the words, "Don't think, don't think" at least twenty times, while concentrating hard on the two words you are repeating. This technique is effective, since it is based on the truth that no one can concentrate on more than one thing at a time. So start today using the "Don't think" to blank your mind of unwanted thought. This procedure will not work right away, but it will prove most effective if you persevere. Use it a thousand times a day. Once you have succeeded in blanking out all thoughts except the thought "Don't think," then consciously direct your thoughts to some other train of thought, preferably something pleasant, like gourmet recipes, for instance. After doing this a thousand or so times a day for several weeks, you will be able to think about the things you want to think about, and will not be at the mercy of thoughts which merely echo your uncontrolled feelings.

You Can Control Your Feelings By Controlling Your Thoughts

I COULD CARE LESS

The "Don't Think" technique is invaluable; it is the heavy artillery in your thought-control arsenal. You might not have to use it when your mental and emotional discomfort is brought on by the minor, trivial, petty, insignificant irritations of daily living. Much of our discomfort is due to the fact that we overreact to trivialities. We allow ourselves to become angry or frightened by things that shouldn't make us angry or fearful. In that case, the quickest and easiest way to rid ourselves of distressing thoughts is to look the situation in the eye and say, with conviction, "It doesn't matter."

Some people use the "Doesn't matter" gambit for serious things. If "Don't think" doesn't work, you might try it on serious problems. But a word of warning: use it only on situations about which you can do nothing. On this basis, that if you can't do anything about it, it really doesn't matter. *Que sera, sera!* Buster or Brat will say, "But darn it, it does matter!'' —His drinking—My mother-in-law taking over. All right, what can you do about it, short of putting Hubby behind bars, or giving Mom arsenic tea? In effect, it doesn't matter. You've got to say to Buster/Brat: "So I could care less!" and put it out of your mind.

So What . . . . . ?!

SELF-DISCIPLINE

If you have an emotional problem and think that some psychologist or psychiatrist or therapist is going to listen to your problem and solve it with a few well-chosen words, you have another think coming. If you have the fond hope that your problem can be resolved painlessly by reading one of many hard-bound $6.95 "Tap-Your-Hidden-Powers Self-Improvement" books with a minimum of effort on your part, you are doomed to disappointment, and will be out $6.95 to boot. The sad fact of the matter is that no therapist or textbook is going to restore your emotional equilibrium for you. No one can do it for you. The therapist or the book may be able to tell you what to do, but in the last analysis, you must do it. This is just another way of saying that regardless of the type of treatment that is suggested, your eventual recovery will depend on self-discipline.

Why is it that so many people who suffer from emotional imbalance are convinced that their problem can be solved without effort on their part, if they can find the person who has the magic formula to impart to them? This is not true of people with physical ailments. If you get sick, you consult the physician. He diagnoses the trouble and prescribes treatment, medication and perhaps a strict regimen of rest, diet, etc. He doesn't "talk" you back to health, and you don't expect him to. You get well by following his orders. This requires self-discipline. If you are diabetic, you force yourself to follow the orders concerning medication and diet. So also if you have an ulcer. If you are a cardiac, you are very careful to observe the lists of DO'S and DON'TS that are laid down for you. You will live to a ripe old age, but only if you do what you are told to do. The doctor cannot do it for you. The same holds true if your malady is emotional; you can be told what is to be done, but you must do it.

Self-Discipline
Is the Basis
Of Emotional Stability
If You Don't Do It,
No One Can
Do It For You.

MAKE THE EFFORT!

It's human nature to substitute thinking and talking for acting. It's so easy to "talk a good game." The key to dealing with an emotional condition is not talk, but action. It doesn't matter what you think; it doesn't matter how you feel; it's what you do that counts! If you suffer from an emotional disorder, you may have been lead to believe that the solution to your problem lies in something called "insight." Insight is Very Big in traditional (so-called modern) psychotherapy. The theory is that in order for you to recover from your emotional disability, you must be given insight into the cause or causes of your condition. Once you determine what it is that has been bugging you, you integrate it into your present life situation and, presto-chango, you're cured. All you have to do is to find the cause of your trouble—the childhood trauma buried deep in your subconscious—and that's it. The beauty of this treatment is that it generally finds a cause in something or someone other than yourself, and more or less absolves you of responsibility for your sad state. It doesn't lay the blame squarely at the door of your controlled feelings and emotions. Unfortunately, it very seldom works. Now, if pinpointing the traumatic experience, making you aware of its nature, and integrating it into your present life-experience doesn't help, what does? Self-discipline. Self-control. Thought-control. Getting the rebellious emotions back in line. That works! Nothing glamorous or mysterious about it. Involves a lot of drudgery, but it works. And after all, that's all that matters.

It Doesn't Matter
What You Think
How You Feel
It's What You Do
That Counts

ANGER

Get angry, but don't "get (go) mad." Somebody said (Confucius maybe?), "The guy who loses his temper loses the argument." Sure, get mad—but don't lose your temper! Losing your temper means losing control. Temper turns into rage, and rage turns you into a dangerous rampaging animal. "Temper" here equals "control." You can't afford to lose it.

Am I saying, "Get mad, but don't let it show?" Indeed not. Let it show if you feel it is justified. State coolly the fact (1) "I am angry—I don't hide this"; (2) "I am angry because . . . " and keep it impersonal: none of this "you stupid so and so, why did you have to go and etc., etc., just when I, etc., etc.!"

The past master of this approach, Haim G. Ginott[1], insists on our being *objective* in selecting the object of our anger: the situation, not the person. Dr. Conrad W. Baars[2] says that anger must not be repressed, but must be expressed in a rational way. Dr. Abraham

Low[3] warns us of the long-fuse effect: you express anger, think it's defused and diffused, and ten minutes later it goes off like a booby trap.

Two good rules to follow in expressing anger: 1) Wait a while (24 hrs?). 2) State it and forget it.

"Next Time, Baby . . . !"

---

[1] Haim G. Ginott, *Between Parent and Child* (Macmillan Co., 1965) and *Between Parent and Teenager* (Macmillan Co., 1969).

[2] Anna A. Terruwe and Conrad W. Baars, *Loving and Curing the Neurotic* (Arlington House, 1972).

[3] Abraham A. Low, *Mental Health Through Will Training* (Boston: Christopher, 1967).

RESENTMENT

Resentment: from the Latin "sentire" (to feel) and "re" (over and over again). Like to take a grievance and turn it over and over and keep the hurt and anger alive? Sure. It's only human. Nice to have a legitimate grievance—makes you feel self-righteous. Makes you feel like *somebody*. Like making bread—you pound the dough and let it rise and pound it again and let it rise. But you don't keep pounding it for a month! (Like the guy who liked pancakes—had five trunks in the attic full of them.)

Resentment is slow poison. It's a psychic heroin addiction. It destroys the mind as surely as heroin destroys the body. It eats away at your peace of mind just as the fox gnawed away at the vitals of the Spartan lad. Want to hug your grudge to your chest? There's a famous man who did just that (name of Benedict Arnold). Express your anger and forget it!

Move Over, Benedict

REVENGE

"Revenge is mine, I will repay, saith the Lord." Revenge is known as cutting off your nose to spite your face or "getting even." On a small scale, it is petty spite.

Ever hear of getting "hoist by your own petard?" (Always thought a petard was some king of a rope with a hook on it. Nope—it's an old time explosive used in the time of Shakespeare.) Somewhat like a modern plastic explosive. Be sure you set the mechanism on the time bomb carefully; the guy you blow up could be you!

Revenge is Sweet,
But It Can Go Sour.

FEAR

Life is just one darn thing after another. Just before you get one fearful problem out of the way, another pops up. Accept the fact that you'll never get caught up, that you'll never be free of fear. In all of history, there never has been anyone who was free of fear except, maybe, Al Capp's "Fearless Fosdick." Remember "The Farmer in the the Dell?" You're the cheese, waiting to be eaten by the rat, who's trying to dodge the cat etc., etc. "Big fleas have little fleas upon their backs to bite 'em; and little fleas have littler fleas and so ad infinitum."

The best way I know of to neutralize a fear was suggested by Willis H. Carrier[4]. In effect, he says that we should imagine the worst as happening and say, "What now?" It works.

A woman came to me who couldn't eat or sleep because she was obsessed with the idea that an atom bomb was going to land in the street. She ran all the way to my office and plopped into the chair all out of breath. So I said, "We'll pretend it's going to go off *right here* at zero. 10, 9, 8, 7, 6, 5, 4, 3, 2, 1, *BOOM!*" I said, "Well?" She said, "We're dead!" I said, "Nice to have it all over, isn't it—especially so quick, like that?" She agreed—and slept and ate well from then on.

Men in combat learn to live and to function with constant fear. One thing they have drilled into them: "Don't panic!" That's the one real danger in fear; it can turn a rational being into a gibbering idiot. Don't ever press the panic button!

Boom!!!! You're Dead!!!!

---

4 Quoted in Dale Carnegie, *How to Stop Worrying and Start Living* (Simon and Shuster, 1948).

ANXIETY

Anxiety seems to be an essential part of the human condition. It's hard to describe—it comes in all shapes and sizes: mild to extreme; particular to general; specific to vague, free-floating, situational, constitutional etc., etc. That's because it's a close stepchild to fear, which can range all the way from mild apprehension to mindless panic.

When we are confronted with a threat—a danger to ourselves or those dear to us—our instinctive reaction is fight or flight; anger or anxiety, or both. These reactions are necessary for self-preservation, but in our complicated society, fighting ("see my lawyer") is generally too complicated, expensive, and time consuming. As to flight, don't try it—they'll trace you! You have only one choice: face up to the fear or anxiety. Do what you can to change the situation. But "situations" can usually be translated "people." It's a pretty generally accepted fact that you can't change people.

If we can't change the situation that causes

the anxiety, we must try to neutralize it. How? By putting it out of our mind—not letting it become an obsession, displacing all our other thoughts. Activity helps. Force yourself to keep busy, especially with physical work or exercise.

As Good Pope John told Cardinal Spellman who called him up in a panic to report that he had a vision of God looking in the window at him: "Looka beezy!"

Damn The Torpedoes, Gridley —Full Speed Ahead!

ENVY

We all admit that in many ways life is a comedy—if we don't go quite as far as Shakespeare and call it a "tale told by an idiot." One of the most comic aspects of life is envy. We all wear masks in public. (The term "personality" originally came from the Greek word for mask.) We can rival secret agents in putting across phony identities. We don't do it on purpose—it just comes natural. But we envy other people's masks and they envy ours.

Envy is silly. It's the silliest feeling you can have. Because you get no bang out of it. You get a certain amount of satisfaction out of blowing your stack in anger; you can get a perverse sort of kick out of self-pity; some people actually enjoy being worrywarts (I suspect); resentment gives a certain type of person a cure for emptiness but tell me, where does envy get you? What's in it for you? We envy a guy because he's rich and we're not. We envy the woman who "has everything." We envy the happy-go-lucky individual who "hasn't a care in the world." We are inclined to envy anyone who (apparently) has something we haven't got. Now the comic thing is that while you're busy envying them, they're busy envying you. That's right, *you!* Why? Because they are making the same mistake about you that you are making about them. They think you've got something they haven't. You're both right, and you're both wrong. Things just ain't what they seem.

Remember Midas? How they all envied him? Until . . . How you envied the lucky guy with the gorgeous wife until you found out his insane jealousy had ruined his every waking moment and brought her to despise and finally hate him! How you envied the boss who gave the lavish presents and threw the greatest parties! (Present address, Danbury Prison, Conn.) Add examples from your own experience. And remember the old story: God led everybody into a storeroom and they all deposited their crosses. Then they went out, and when they came back in, He told everyone to pick out just the cross he wanted for himself—get the best fit possible. Know what? Of course! Everyone came out with the cross he had brought in.

*Grass Is Always
Greener On The
Other Side of the Fence.
But After You Climb The
Fence: Which Is The
"Other" Side?*

(with Apologies to Zen).

THE "PLOM" SYNDROME

Self-pity is for the birds. They eat worms. So do fish. OK for them—but not for you. "Nobody loves me—I'm going out into the garden and eat worms!" "They'll be sorry when they stand by my casket and see me all laid out!"

"I'll run away from home—if I can get a nice crossing guard to cross me!" "I'm too fat! They laugh at me!" —Weightwatchers or TOPS will just love you to pieces! "I'm ugly!"—So was Lincoln. "They laugh at the way I talk!" Ever hear of Sam Goldwyn? Casey Stengel? P. L. O. M.! (Poor Little Old Me!) —Kid stuff! ("Here: mommy'll kiss the nasty old bump and everything will be all right.")

Try Growing Up

INADEQUATE?

Do you feel inadequate—part of the time, some of the time, or most of the time? You do? Glad to hear it—you're an average human being. I suspect that everybody's born with a sense of inadequacy that persists for a lifetime—self-mistrust, inferiority feeling, inadequacy—call it what you will. Sort of a universal birth defect. The ironic thing about it is that the people who feel inadequate seldom are, and the people (rare) who feel totally adequate turn out to be just the opposite.

Feelings to the contrary notwithstanding, anybody who is not severely mentally handicapped and/or physically incapacitated can do anything anybody else can do. For example, years ago I met a young woman just out of a State Hospital, whose husband had disappeared with their three small children. Frances was completely untrained for any position. She went from nurse's aide to practical nurse to R.N. to B. S., to Medical Nursing Practitioner. She is now in a key position in a large city clinic. Yes, she located her husband and children. Needless to say they are proud of their mother—as is the prestigious and very selective university which subsidized her graduate work and granted her degrees.

There are thousands like her. But to mention another of my favorites: in a like situation this lady parlayed her only apparent talent, cake baking, into a job on a university campus as pastry cook—then as dietitian, then as head of a dining room, then as the head of the university food program. Needless to say, Adele's kids are proud of her, as is the university which provided her the courses she needed to get to the top. Every time I see her I have an almost irrepressible urge to say, "Bake me a six-foot cake with *you* on top!"

Feel Inadequate?
—Shame On You!

MOOD SWINGS
(UPS & DOWNS)

Would it surprise you to know that the average person has at least four, more often, five bad days a month—man, woman and child? It surprised me, when I first read about it in *Is This Your Day?*[5]

As a matter of fact, if you were born on a Wednesday, every other Wednesday will be a "bad day" for the rest of your life! Mood swings are a fact of life, a part of living. You'd better acknowledge them and use them. On good days, everything seems to break right for you. You enjoy. So enjoy! Sing a little. Act a little foolish. Be a little manic. Put a silly grin on your face. "Gather ye rosebuds while ye may."

Then the bad days. You know as you stub your toe on the way to the bathroom that this is going to be "one of those days," and that's the way it turns out. Everything that can go wrong, does. The rule to follow on these days is to keep your mouth shut. Confine your remarks to "Hi!" (Say anything further and you'll wind up jobless, wifeless and maybe lifeless.)

Meanwhile nuts to trying to think happy thoughts. It's phony and besides, it just makes things worse. Act natural; don't cry on anybody's shoulder, but don't try to be a little ray of sunshine, either. Say to yourself, "I'm miserable. So I feel miserable. So what else is new?" It'll go away! Accept the misery, and try not to let it show. You can stick it out till bedtime.

Life At Best Is No Bargain: Enjoy The Ups Tough Out the Downs

---

[5] George Thommen, *Is This Your Day?* (Univ. Pub. and Dist., 1968).

DEPRESSION

Note: you Earth People who have never suffered a clinical, chronic pathological depression, thank God and skip this section.

You stay up as late as you can at night, because you dread the agony of waking up after a few hours' fitful sleep. That waking moment is the worst. That's when the guts knot tighter: "O God, I can't make it through another day! If I stay in bed, I'll toss and turn for four more hours. I don't want to get up, but I might as well." Go through the motions. Drag my drained-out self through another day. Can't eat. Getting to be a living skeleton. This damned rock where my stomach used to be. Putting on the act: "How are you?" "Just fine!" Getting behind and pushing, pushing, pushing. Try the amateur cures. "Go someplace!" Tried it. No good. "Try booze." Did. Made it worse. Well, what then? Accept it. Fight it. Tough it out. Keep breathing. And know that it will come to an end. It always has before and it will again. Someday I'll feel good—just a little. As a matter of fact, maybe I feel just a bit good today. Afraid to believe it though, can't afford to get my hopes up. Probably just an illusion. Wait. Wake up this morning—could it be? This afternoon, good feeling was still there. It's *true*! Lord, how good it feels to feel good!

Until that blessed moment comes, fight it. Don't give in. Say "I feel miserable, so OK, I feel miserable." Chant it as you force yourself to do all the impossible things that are expected of you. Go to work. Work. Or get the meals, dress the kids, wash the clothes, clean the house, as the case may be. Force yourself! Don't give in. Or, OK, give in! Sit in the middle of the floor and cry. "I can't go on!" OK, but you'll have to get up sometime.

You have to do the fighting, but there are good, effective chemicals that will help you fight. They won't do it for you, but they'll help you fight. See the MD. Get them. Use them. Surrender to the fact that you're miserable; but that far, and no farther. Remember: it isn't how you feel, it's what you *do* that counts. And it won't be forever.

If you and God are on good terms, don't ask Him to cure you; ask Him to help you live with it until it goes away. Meanwhile, offer up to Him your agony. It's the highest form of prayer. All pain is precious; don't waste it. It will come back from Him as blessing on you and—more important—on yours. If you would like to see a fuller treatment of this subject, see "Grief."[6]

THIS TOO WILL PASS

---

[6] Vincent P. Collins, *Grief* (Abbey Press, 1966).

COMPULSION
("The Devil Made Me Do It!")

Some people are obsessive-compulsive; that is, they are obsessed by an idea which drives every other thought out of their mind—it is King of the Hill. Or they perform actions which they don't want to perform but are powerless not to perform. Crazy stuff like washing your hands every fifteen minutes—kicking the tires before you get in to drive—checking the doors, the stove, the water faucets, the refrigerator, the windows three times before you leave the house, etc., etc. All the time saying, "This is nuts, but I can't help it."

An obsession takes over the mind. A compulsion takes over the will, at least in one particular area. The will becomes paralyzed, in a sense. It just can't function in the face of the compulsion. The only way to overcome this condition is to do what people do whose muscles are temporarily inoperative after an operation. Try P. T. In their case, that means

"Physio-Therapy." In yours, "Push Therapy." Get behind and push. Physio-therapy means "make with the muscles." Push therapy, really. Mental PT is the same—make with the muscles—or do you want to be confined to a mental wheel chair the rest of your life?

By the way, Recovery Incorporated helps a lot for this, as well as for any nervous ailment. They're in the white pages. Why not give them a call?

FREEDOM NOW!

PHOBIAS

In creating you, God intended that your actions should be controlled by your intellect and not by your imagination and your emotions. No matter how strongly you feel to the contrary, you can control your actions. When you have trained yourself to control your thoughts, you will find that you can also control your impulses to action. This despite the fact that you may have persistent obsessions or deep-rooted phobias. If you are obsessed by a certain train of thought to such an extent that you cannot seem to think of anything else, no matter how hard you try, you are the victim of an obsession. We have stated above that you can get to control your thoughts, to turn them off and on like a faucet. You can accomplish this by the unflagging use of the "don't think" technique. This condition obtains in the realm of action as well as thought. For instance, if you have a fear, or phobia, of germs, you may have a corresponding impulse to wash your hands every five minutes. This is called a compulsion. What obsession is to thought, compulsion is to action. Just as obsession can be conquered by the use of the will, so also compulsions will yield to the persevering use of the will. (There is one important exception to this, however. A compulsion with a physical dependence, such as an addiction to a drug, will not yield to willpower. But that is another story.) Phobias can be overcome in only one way: consistently and doggedly disregarding them and acting against them, no matter how uncomfortable it may make you feel. Just as one gradually gets control of rebellious thoughts by forcing himself to think about something else, so one can also gain mastery over irrational phobias by forcing himself to act against the impulses they give rise to.

Fear of heights is one of the most common of the phobias. Suppose you would rather walk up twenty-five flights than take an elevator, or "wouldn't be caught dead taking a plane." How do you overcome it? Quit giving in to it. Act against it. Take the elevator. If you faint, they'll pick you up. Take the plane—if you turn green, the pretty hostess will hold your hand and make sympathetic noises. But at any rate DO IT! Giving in to a phobia or a compulsion strengthens it. Resisting it conquers it.

*Force Yourself To Do
What You Are
Afraid To Do. Giving In
Intensifies Phobias:
Resisting Overcomes Them*

MAKE WITH THE MUSCLES!

The operative word is "force yourself!" Get behind and push. Suppose you suffer from emotional fatigue. Everything is a terrible effort. You feel drained, exhausted, "bushed," from the moment you get up in the morning until you drag yourself to bed at night. You feel like taking up permanent residence in bed. (I know several victims of nervous fatigue who spend days and days, especially weekends, in bed. Interviewing one depressed person, I asked her, "Do you take to your bed on weekends, when you are not working?" "No," she answered. "Good for you!" I said. But I spoke too soon; she finished, "I stay in the tub!")

If you must force yourself to do things, to what extent do you have to force yourself? How far do you have to go? A simple, common-sense rule of thumb is this: never force yourself to do more than would be expected of the average person in your situation, but at the same time, don't fail to do anything that would be expected of the average person in your situation. In other words, don't let your feelings keep you from doing what is reasonably to be expected of you, but at the same time, don't try to do more than would be expected of the average person in your situation, just to prove something. You don't have to prove anything to anyone, even to yourself. For example, if you are a housewife, never excuse yourself from doing all the things that a housewife should do; if you are a salesman, get out and make the route regardless of how you feel. In short, don't give in to yourself. "Feet, do your stuff!"

*Never Fail To Do Anything
That is Reasonably
To Be Expected of You,
Even If You Have
To Force Yourself.
Never Do More Than Is
Reasonably To Be Expected,
Just to Prove Something*

BOOZE

Friend or Foe?
Drinking more this year than last year at
this time?
Thinking constantly about your next
drink?
No longer able to joke about a hangover?
Wondering if tonight's the night you're
going to go overboard?
Beginning to pray, "Dear Lord, don't let
me drink too much this time!?"
Unable to guarantee your behavior after
the first drink?
Wife/husband/boss/client/foreman
beginning to give hints?
A little fuzzy about how you got home last
night?

Maybe you ought to look into it.—"Maybe,"
nuts! Get out the white pages and call AA!

THREE NO-NO'S:

"Young man, don't ever let me hear you
say
    1. WHY?!
    2. IF ONLY!!
    3. WHAT IF???
or I'll wash your mouth out with soap!"
"Yes, mother!"

WHY?

Why anything? As Doc Green of Detroit and Brighton (Michigan)—a very wise old coot (his own expression)—used to say: "If a guy came into Receiving with a broken arm I didn't put him on a couch, whip out a note-book, and ask him if he a) fell on a rollerskate on the stairs b) tripped over the cat, c) slipped on a banana peel, d) etc. etc. No! I X-rayed the arm and set it. My philosophy is not 'how did you get this way?' but 'what do we do?' And I proceeded to do it. And that goes for nuts and drunks (his expression) as well as broken bones."

The most useless question is, "Why do they (people) act that way?" There's a very simple answer: "because they're people!" And that's all you have to know.

People Will Be People!

IF ONLY . . .

"If wishes were horses, beggars would ride!" One of the hallmarks of emotional maturity is the ability to take reality as it is. Conversely, wishful thinking is one of the indications of immaturity as an indirect refusal to accept one's situation. A subtle tip-off to it is the "If only" thing. Like, "If only I had played my hunch on Dandy Lion in the sixth, instead of that dog, the 1-5 favorite, I'da been in $400 bucks!" "If only I took that tip on Lunatronics in 1944 I'd be worth $40,500,000 today!" "If only I had married that dame from Cape Cod." Etc., etc., etc. Well, you didn't! Dandy Lion would have thrown the jock at the gate, Lunatronics would have turned out to be wallpaper, and that dame would've turned out to be Lucretia Borgia, reincarnated. Fella, you just can't win!

So cut it out—if you can't get what you like (who does?), you'd better like what you've got.

WHAT IF?

The worrywart's slogan: "What if . . . ?" "What if we go bankrupt?" "What if my husband drops dead?" (Well, lady . . . !) "What if the IRS audits me?" (They did me, and I'll never be afraid of them again.) "What if the Rock of Gibraltar turns into Jello?" "What if Niagara Falls runs dry?" (It did once, due to an icejam, but it's back in business.) "What if Junior flunks math?" (Why not, Einstein did). "What if the sky falls?" (Ask Chicken Little.) "What if, what if, what if?"

So what can you do about it? Wait and see. Stop crossing bridges etc.—they'll invent something to take care of it. Or, as they say in the Bronx, "You should live so long!"

WORD TO THE WISE:
NEED HELP?

—RECOVERY, INC.—
Try It, You'll Like It.

—AA—
Try It—They'll Like You

(In The White Pages)

SELF-APPROVAL

We know that for you to live comfortably with yourself, you have to be able to approve of yourself. That is, you have to be able to accept yourself and to feel worthwhile. In the last analysis, living comfortably depends not on the good opinion of others, but on one's own good opinion of one's self. How many times do you find yourself asking, "What will my husband (mother, friend, etc.) think?" instead of "What do I think?" It is a sign of the mature person to seek advice of others, but to make the final decision on one's own. If you try to please everybody, you wind up pleasing nobody, not even yourself.

*The Fundamental Basis
For Comfortable Living
Is Merited Self-Approval*

WORTHWHILE

To determine whether or not you are worthwhile to yourself and others, it is absolutely essential to determine first of all what is to be reasonably expected of you by yourself and others. The easiest way to determine that is to determine what is expected of the average person in your situation. Once you have determined what you would expect of the average person, make that your norm. Expect no more and no less of yourself. If you are undecided as to what is expected of you, pretend that you are someone else, and see what you would expect of him. Pick out someone in your neighborhood of the same age, sex, marital status and standard of living and decide what you would expect him to do if he were in your situation. Then expect no more and no less of yourself. By removing yourself mentally from the situation and looking at it from the outside, you will come up with a reasonable course of action. Once you have

determined what can reasonably be expected
of you, go ahead and do it.

Determine What Is
Reasonably To Be Expected
Of the Average Person
And Try To Measure
Up To It

YOU OWE IT TO YOURSELF

You owe it to your family, friends, and community to do what is expected of you, but above all, you owe it to yourself. For your own peace of mind and contentment, you must measure up to your obligations. Do what is expected of you not to gain the approval of someone else, but to gain your own approval. Do it not for the sake of someone else, but for your own sake. Let's forget for the moment about our relationship with others and look at it from the point of view of self-interest. Regardless of what your duties to others may be, you owe it first and foremost to yourself to produce. Nothing contributes so much to our feeling of well-being as the satisfaction of doing something worthwhile. Likewise, nothing can make us so uncomfortable as a sense of unworthiness or self-disgust that comes when we fall down on the job, letting ourselves down. We owe it to ourselves to be able to feel worthwhile.

You Owe It
To Yourself
To Measure Up

LIMITS

One thing should be made clear: we can never violate the genuine rights of others in doing what pleases ourselves. There are limits. No one can seriously advocate that you should go through life without regard for the sensibilities of others. Your own self-interest demands such a regard, simply because you have learned from experience that in deliberately hurting another's feelings, you are hurting yourself. You certainly can't swashbuckle your way through life like a Caribbean buccaneer, leaving a swath of wounded and hurt sensibilities in your wake. You have no right to say or do anything that would be justly resented by others. But at the same time, the principle holds that in considering a course of action, you should not be swayed by consideration of an unreasonable or unwarranted emotional reaction on the part of others. Others expect you to react reasonably to what they say or do; certainly you have the same right in relation to them. If something you do or say "hurts their feelings" without cause, their reaction is unreasonable. Disregard it. It's their problem, not yours.

"Do Unto Others. . . ."

AVERAGENESS

One of the greatest aids to peace of mind is the concept of averageness. If we can get it through our heads that we are average people, we can spare ourselves a lot of grief. To the untutored eye, one daisy is much like any other daisy. There are individual differences, to be sure, but in the main, one daisy is much like any other daisy. Daisies share a common nature; they have the same physical makeup and the same range of capabilities. The same holds true, in general, of human beings. We share a common nature. We have the same general appearance and the same general capacities and capabilities. We are ordinary, average members of the human race. In the things that really count, you and I are no better and no worse, no more or less capable, than the average person. What they can do, we can do; and what we can do, they can do.

Keep in Mind
The Fact That
You Are An
Average Human Being

FALLIBILITY

You are Mr. and Mrs. Average Person. In the main, you react in much the same way as any other person to heat and cold, pleasure and pain, work and leisure, sickness and health. Things that bug the average person generally bug you. From this basic consideration, you can draw three conclusions that will be of inestimable help to your peace of mind. First, being average, you have no right to hold too high an opinion of yourself. You shouldn't be chagrined if you are not 100% efficient, 100% omniscient, 100% perfect. Second, being average, you shouldn't allow yourself to have too low an opinion of yourself. That is, you must believe that you are as capable as the average person. Finally, being average, you shouldn't feel that you are better than the average person, that you deserve more from life than anyone else and have a right to go through life exempt from the usual "ills that flesh is heir to," such as pain, suffering, reverses and the rest of the things that can make life difficult.

It's No Crime
Not To Be Perfect

GIVE YOURSELF A BREAK

You can be too hard on yourself. One of the real threats to your peace of mind is the natural inclination to demand more of yourself than you do of others, even to demand more of yourself than others demand of you. For instance, many people are upset because they can't come right up with the answer to a simple question such as, "Name the presidents," or "Give the state capitals." Nobody is expected to know everything, you included. Nobody is expected to do a perfect job in any area, you included. Everyone "goofs" occasionally, you included. And it is not usually a federal offense to make mistakes. Let's get away from the silly idea that it's a disgrace not to be perfect. Much more comfortable making mistakes and admitting them.

Maybe you're a victim of the "FF Syndrome" (Fear of Failure). So what? Everyone else is. Trouble is, you think you're the only one who has it. Everyone has it, to some degree. But they don't let it paralyze them. Maybe you'll fail. So did Columbus—he never did get to India!

YOU CAN DO IT

You can sell yourself short. This is especially true if you live with someone who is constantly pointing out your real or fancied shortcomings to build up his or her own deficient ego. You can, after years of this treatment, get to believe that you are not as capable as the average person, that you're "not much good at anything." Don't you believe it! What the average person can do, you can do—maybe not as well as some, but well enough to get by. If they can do it, you can do it. Your judgment, for instance, is as good as the average person's, and better than some; trust it. If there's something you would like to try to do, pitch in and try it. Who knows, you may well have hidden talents that neither you nor anyone else suspected. You never know until you try.

If They Can Do It,
I Can Do It

WHY ME?

No one likes to admit that he is "just average." In your secret heart of hearts, you would like to believe that you are someone special, exceptional. Up to a point, this is true. It is not true, however, that you, be you special or average, have a right to be exempt from suffering what the average person suffers. You have no right, really, to ask "Why me?" when you suffer misfortune. "Why me, of all people?", the inference being that you, because of your exceptional endowment of mind, spirit and body, don't deserve the fate of common mortals. Or that you, because of your blameless life and great service to your fellowman, should be spared any kind of pain and suffering. Why you, of all people? Rather, why not you, of all people? What makes you so special? It may be uncomfortable for you to face up to the fact that you have no right to immunities denied the average person, but the fact remains that you are an "average person." You will never live comfortably with yourself until you get realistic, come to terms with life as it is, and admit the fact that you are an average person.

Accept the Fact That You Are No Better Than Anyone Else

UNIQUE

At this point, we must give some attention to one of the paradoxes of the human personality. We have been belaboring the point that you are exactly like everyone else. You are unique. You are a human being, but you are not just any human being. In all the history of mankind there never has been, nor will ever be a person exactly like you. You have feelings and thoughts that no one else has ever felt or thought before. You have a unique dignity: of all the millions of people that God might have created in place of you, he chose to create you. Because you are unique, no one else can know exactly how you feel or what you think; nor can you ever know exactly how another feels or what he thinks. No one can really understand any other being. For that matter, you can't really understand yourself!

It is comforting to realize that no human being can fully understand any other human being. This is particularly true of married people. A myth has sprung up to the effect that marital partners, in order to live together in peace and harmony, must "understand" each other. Efforts to achieve this mutual understanding can lead to complete frustration. "But I can't understand him!" So who says you have to? "But he doesn't understand me!" Why should he? For any close relationship to be successful, it is not necessary that the individuals understand what makes each other tick; but it is essential that they respect each other and accept each other as they are.

*Accept the Fact
That No One Can
Really Understand You
And That You Can't
Really Understand
Any Other Human Being*

PART II

ME VS. YOU

"INSIGHT"

The fact that no human being can fully understand any other human being can be of comfort to anyone who suffers from an emotional illness. Unfortunately, you may share the prevalent opinion that in order to be helped, you must be understood, and that in order to help another person, you must be able to understand him. It is quite generally believed today that the therapist must figure out from his patient's history how the patient "got that way." Having attained this insight, he directly passes the insight on to the patient. Lately, however, there is a growing tendency on the part of practitioners to forget "how you got this way" in favor of "what to do about it." If you break an arm, healing it in no way depends on knowing whether you slipped on a banana peel or on a roller skate or whatever. The very same is true of emotional broken arms and hearts: it doesn't matter how you got that way, it's what you do about it that counts! The solution to any emotional problem consists not in finding out what caused it, but in determining what is to be done about it, and doing it.

Forget "Insight."
Who Needs It?

PEOPLE

Up to now, we have been considering how your feelings can affect your emotional well-being. The next step will be to consider how other people can affect the way you feel. Later on, we will take up the question of how other people can affect not only the way you feel, but also the way you act.

How can other people affect the way you feel? It all depends on how you let them affect you. They can make you happy or miserable, if you let them. At the very outset you must accept this proposition as true: it is not our situation that makes us happy or miserable, it's the way in which we react to it. Look around at some of your friends. You will notice that Joe is as miserable as can be in a situation that would make Jim happy as a lark, and Eleanor is radiantly happy in a situation that would send Beatrice to the Funny Farm. So it's not our situation itself that is to blame for our unhappiness; it's our reaction to it. When we talk about a "situation," we generally mean "people." When we talk about our situation in terms of "good" or "bad," we really mean that our reaction to the people we are associated with is "good" or "bad," that is, pleasant or unpleasant. We react to what people say and do. We react either to what they are doing to themselves, or closer to home, what they are doing to us. In the first instance, we may be unhappy at what they are doing, even though it does not affect us directly. This is the case if you have a grown son who is making a fool of himself. In the second instance, we may be unhappy because of what someone is doing to us. This is the case if you have an insanely jealous husband or a neurotic or alcoholic wife. In any case, you are letting someone make you unhappy.

Do you let people bug you? Does your happiness depend upon what others think or say about you, or how they treat you? Do you care a great deal about the way your friends and relatives think about you, talk about you and treat you? Or even the way in which they might possibly think about you? Do you find yourself saying, "I don't care what people think!" when all the time you care very much what they think? If you are an average person, you firmly believe that other people can hurt your feelings. You may be convinced that your state of mind depends to a great extent on whether other people, especially those close to

you, approve or disapprove of you. If this is
the way you feel, you have lots of company.
Bad company!

It Isn't Your
Situation That Makes
You Sad Or Glad
It's Your
Reaction to it

"SWEET ALICE"

If this is the way it is with you, you have a patron saint. She is "Sweet Alice." Never heard of her? She was the heroine of a popular Victorian ballad entitled "Sweet Alice, Ben Bolt." It went like this: "Do you remember sweet Alice, Ben Bolt? Sweet Alice with hair so brown! Who would laugh with delight if you gave her a smile, and tremble with fear at your frown." The Sweet Alice laugh and tremble philosophy of life is all too prevalent. There are all too many "Sweet Alices." And unfortunately, a great many are married to immature, neurotic, egocentric or alcoholic spouses, or working for a boss who is demanding, unappreciative, thoughtless or just plain mean. If this is the case with you, you're in trouble. You are living in reaction to others. Your happiness depends on a person who is incapable of making you happy. Anyone whose happiness is at the mercy of someone else is usually unhappy. No one can afford to let his peace of mind depend on anyone other than himself. If you can't bring yourself to agree with this, be my guest. Alice, have a few trembles on me!

You Alone Can Make
Or Break
Your Peace of Mind

HURT FEELINGS

Are you one of those people who bruise easily? Whose feelings are always getting hurt? Well, then, it's time you learned that it isn't the way other people treat you that can hurt your feelings, but the way you react to their treatment. It's your reaction, not their action, that counts. When you say, "But they hurt my feelings!" what you really mean is "I let my feelings be hurt." Actually, no one can hurt your feelings unless you let them. You can't control what they say or do, but you most certainly can control the way you react to what they say or do. How? By training yourself to ignore anything that isn't reasonable. By refusing to think about it. By letting it go in one ear and out the other. By saying "It doesn't matter!" "Easier said than done." Yes, that's true, but it can be done. Here's one way of doing it: imagine yourself comfortably situated inside a big plexiglass bubble, completely insulated from all the irresponsible or unreasonable things people say or do to you.

The words and deeds bounce right off the surface of your transparent igloo. They can't get at you unless you put down one of two gangways to admit them. One gangway is marked "Anger" and the other is marked "Fear." Nobody can let them in but you, and only by way of resentment or worry. Try it, and you'll see!

Nobody Can Hurt Your Feelings Unless You Let Them

BOYS WILL BE BOYS

"But it isn't right! It isn't fair! People shouldn't say such things!" You're so right; of course it isn't fair, and they shouldn't. But that's the way it is, and that's the way it's going to be. Things are tough all over! There just ain't no justice in this life. You're absolutely right. But where does that get you? Boys will be boys, and people will be people. There's nothing you or I or anybody can do about it. So ignore it. Forget it. And for Pete's sake, stop saying "But people shouldn't do this and people shouldn't say that." Gets pretty monotonous.

Along this line, I like the story about the two psychiatrists. It seems they were going up in the elevator at the Medical Center. As they approached the sixth floor, the operator bowed to one of them and said, "Your floor, Doctor," and opened the door. "Thank you," said he, leaning over and biting the ear of the other psychiatrist. Then he stepped off the elevator and walked jauntily down the corridor to his office. Open mouthed, the operator looked over at the remaining psychiatrist, who was quietly standing there with the blood dripping down onto his jacket. "Say, Doc," he inquired, "Aren't you going to do something about that?" "Why should I?" answered the other. "He's the one who's got the problem!"—Think it over. The Doc is right. It isn't the person who has to put up with unreasonable or irresponsible behavior that has the problem, it's the person who is acting unreasonably or irresponsibly that really has the problem. He is the one who needs help.

Find Out Who's Got the Problem

CRITICISM

No one is immune to criticism. Everybody makes mistakes. And if you don't make mistakes, you'll get criticized for not making mistakes. You just can't win. Never expect to be understood, much less appreciated, above all to be thanked. But do expect to be criticized. Like the philanthropist who met one of his beneficiaries on the street. The latter was noticeably cool in greeting his benefactor. "What's the matter, Sam? Thought you'd be glad to see me. After all, I bailed out your business, kept your wife from leaving you, talked the bank out of foreclosing your mortgage and saved your boy from reform school." To which Sam replied, "Yeah, but what have you done for me lately?" It seems that you just can't please some people. And no matter what you do, you'll always be criticized.

Do you get all shook up when you are the victim of unjust criticism? Most people do. But they're mistaken. The only time you should get shook up is when there's a kernel of truth in the criticism. "The truth hurts." When the criticism isn't true, don't get mad; thank God it isn't true and pray for the one who is doing the criticizing. He's got a problem. If there does happen to be some truth in the criticism, get mad. Don't get mad at the critic; get mad at yourself and resolve not to lay yourself open to criticism again.

Pay No Attention Whatsoever,
Internally or Externally,
To Anything That Anyone
Says or Does To You
Or About You That Is
In Your Own Honest,
Objective Opinion,
Untrue, Unjust,
Unreasonable or Exaggerated

TWO OPINIONS

I omitted this section from the first edition of *ME, MYSELF, and YOU* because my friends said it sounded arrogant, vain, etc. etc. At first glance it does. But it happens to be true. Further, they said, it could easily be misinterpreted to mean, "nuts to what anybody else thinks!" Which also is true. (One of the occupational hazards of counseling is that each party may twist what the counselor says into an argument for "his side." Well, that's the nature of the beast.)

The principle is this: in the last analysis, there are only two opinions in the world that should matter to me: mine and God's. That is, my own *merited* self-approval and God's approval. If I am honestly sure that my course of action is truly the best for me and for everyone concerned, and at the same time does not violate the law of God, then I should not be swayed by the opinion of others. Once more, I must not live in reaction to the actual or anticipated reaction of others to my behavior.

If I am in a position of authority, the first thing I should get is a bullet-proof vest. Then I must remember the undying, immortal words of Harry S Truman, "If you can't stand the heat, get out of the kitchen!"

Have The Courage of Your Convictions.

EXPLANATIONS

Live your own life! Never mind seeking the approval of other people, whoever they may be. Do your very best to live up to your own standards, and try to earn your own self-approval. Make your decisions to the best of your ability and then stand by them. Before you act, don't worry about how the unreasonable, the hypercritical, the hypersensitive, the hysterical or the immature are going to take your action. After you have acted, don't expect the approval of the unreasonable, the immature, the envious. Above all, don't prolong the agony by trying to explain to your critics why you did what you did. Trying to "explain" to someone who just can't or won't accept an explanation is a waste of time. It makes matters worse. It's like sending good money after bad. Trying to explain or justify your action merely dignifies the irresponsible criticism. It gives the impression that you are taking the irresponsible criticism seriously, as perhaps you are. Forget it! And that goes for the practice of defending yourself to yourself. That is, making up little speeches in your head in which you list all the reasons why you were right in doing what you did. Life's too short. Stop making silent speeches and rebuttals as you drive to the supermarket. This deplorable practice not only intensifies your discomfort, but, according to the National Safety Council, it can also cause accidents.

Never Dignify Unfair Criticism by Trying To Explain or Defend Yourself, Even to Yourself

IS YOUR SOUL YOUR OWN?

To live and let live means to live your own life and let others live theirs. Living your own life is the opposite of the Sweet Alice Syndrome, which is living in reaction, that is, letting other people live your life for you. We have seen that you can allow other people to dictate your state of mind by overreacting to their opinion of your words and actions, by rejoicing at their approval and being dejected by their disapproval. This is what you do, in effect, if you belong to the "Life-Is-a-Popularity-Contest" school of thought. This is bad enough, since it allows others to determine how you feel; but you can even go a step further and allow them to determine not only how you feel, but also what you do. This is precisely what you are doing when you decide a course of action not on the basis of what is best for you, but on the basis of how others will react to it. You are allowing your actions, as well as your feelings, to be determined by the anticipated reaction of others. So your soul is not your own! If in planning something your prime consideration is, "How is Tom, Dick, Harry or Mother going to take this?" you are not running your life. Tom, Dick, Harry or Mother is. Not in the sense that they are baldly ordering you to do this or not to do that. With a Sweet Alice, they don't have to. They just use the "Smile and Frown" technique, and your sensitivity enables them to get away with it. Everyone knows the Martyred-Mother Matriarch type who runs the lives of her married children by the Heart Attack or Dizzy Spell technique. There's one in every neighborhood. It would be better if she used a gun—more honest, at any rate. But remember, it won't work if you don't go along with it.

In short, if you are a Sweet Alice, your happiness is out of your control because it depends not on your own judgment, your own will, your own choice but on the judgment, will and choice of the person to whom you are living in reaction. A good case in point is that of the wife of a jealous husband. She has made a practice of doing nothing that might "make him mad," to "keep peace in the family." When he ordered her to turn over the shopping to him (because, he said, she was having an affair with the man at the meat counter), she did so. When he forbade the insurance man to come to the house to collect the premium, she went along with it. When he ordered her not to make or receive calls on the phone, she went along with it. She also "went along with it" when he ordered her to quit bowling, to give up the Home Bureau meetings and the church affairs. And the afternoon cup of coffee with her married sister down the street. She went along with these insanities and many more. She went right along with everything—right into the State Hospital.

"Nice Guys" Come In Last

LOVE'S LABOR LOST

Good old Sweet Alice! You might justify the sacrifice of her autonomy if it had accomplished anything, but it didn't. It not only didn't help, it actually made matters worse for herself and for her husband. They would both have been better off if she had defied him. If you live with a person with an obvious emotional problem, you won't help things by giving in to him, "humoring him." This will merely serve to aggravate his problem and finally drive you to the wall. If you ignore his nonsense, at least you retain your own sanity and you may help him to recover. No one maintains that this is easy, because it obviously is not, but it is the only thing to do. You must act according to your convictions and choose your course of action on the sole basis of what seems best to you. Let him rant and rave until he's hoarse, but pay no attention. What is best for you in your honest considered opinion will generally prove to be best for all concerned. "What's good for General Motors is good for the country."

Act, Don't React
Live Your Own Life!

GUILTY!

Too many people in families, clubs, businesses and government think you can solve a problem by finding out "who's to blame?" (Fat lot of good that does, e.g., after an official sixth month's NAA investigation into a horrific plane crash.)

If you really want to know, in most interpersonal clashes everybody's to blame and nobody's to blame. Using the "who's to blame?" technique makes family problems worse, and in corporation and governmental bureaucracies it has a paralyzing effect; no one will take responsibility for a course of action because he may be "blamed." So he does nothing, or passes the buck. (Exception: Harry S Truman—"The buck stops here.")

In any situation that demands immediate action, don't waste precious time asking "who's to blame?" Ask, "What do we do about it, here and now?"—That's better!

They Just Found Out Who Was To Blame For The Titanic *And The* Hindenberg

BONUS

After you screw up the courage to do what you want to do regardless of how someone else is going to react to it, you will begin to collect bonuses. For instance, people who have gotten in the habit of taking you for granted are going to rediscover you as an individual. They are going to respect you; the doormat has gotten off the floor and started acting like a human being. Better yet, you are going to begin to respect yourself. You will be able to take full responsibility for your actions. If you make mistakes, as you certainly will, at least you will have the comfort of knowing that they are your own mistakes. You made them out of conviction, not just to please someone, to keep the peace, or out of expediency. You will have the satisfaction of knowing that you are doing what you really want to do, not what someone else wants you to do. You have acquired the greatest bonus of all: the courage to make mistakes. In the immortal words of Farragut, "Damn the torpedoes, full steam ahead!"

Have the Courage
To Make Mistakes

COMMUNICATION

One of the current buzz-words very much in vogue between husbands and wives, parents and children, and bosses and workers is "COMMUNICATION." (Very big in current magazine psychology, too.) "We can't communicate!" is the universal wail. Or, in business and industry: "The lines of communication seem to have broken down."

Maybe so; but just let's recall a simple truth: communication is lacking when the communicator can't or won't make himself clear and or the communicatee can't or won't listen. Ever try to talk to someone who is just waiting for you to stop talking so he can start? Hasn't heard a word you said.

What to do about the communication problem? If you are trying to get something across, get it straight in your own mind first; don't go off half-cocked. Express what you mean in clear language. (A friend of mine who has 5 Ph.D's in various branches of science says that any man who really knows his subject can explain any abstruse theory from atomic energy to relativity in layman's language.) If a book confuses you (this one, for instance), it's not because you're confused—the author is.

If you are the communicatee, let down the mental barricades erected by your feelings and open your mind as well as your ears. Don't put words in the other person's mouth or thoughts in his head. ("I know what you think!" "—The heck you do!") You only know what I think when I tell you what I think. When you try to guess what someone else is thinking or feeling, you generally guess wrong. If you want to know what I think or feel don't guess—ask me and I'll tell you. I'll return the favor.

Talk Straight—Listen Good Avoid Guesstimates

DISCUSSION—OR ARGUMENT?

From time immemorial, ancient custom dictates that there are two subjects that are taboo in a bar, even in, or perhaps especially in, Scolly's Square (of happy memory). They are a) religion and b) politics. Why? Because it seems that these subjects defy rational discussion, generate more heat than light, and sometimes result in a donnybrook. Because they involve feelings, emotions. Feelings are the enemy of rational discussion. This can be particularly true of discussions between husband and wife.

The formula for discussion vs. argument is simple: State what you think coolly and unemotionally. Give reasons for your views and let it lay there. Invite the other person to do the same. Don't interrupt. And by all means have it understood that you are not attempting to convince him that you are right and insist on the same privilege: you have no obligation to agree that he is right. About as far as you can go—the ultimate outer limits—would be to say "I think you are mistaken." One more thing: never resort to personalities—discuss the question, not the person. And for the sake of peace and quiet, never (this applies to old married people) but *never* bring up the past! The water's under the bridge and over the dam. And we know that it won't run backward. Yesterday is history; and as Santayana said, man learns from history that man learns nothing from history.

No Donnybrooks!

ACTION, NOT REACTION

It may take you a while to stop reacting and start acting. Further, if you have been letting someone else—a mother or husband—run your life for a long time, the confrontation will take a great deal of courage. But go ahead, and let the chips fall where they may. When the unreasonable criticism comes, ignore it. For example, suppose that you buy something that is absolutely necessary for the family, such as groceries. When your better half, who considers any money not spent on booze to be a dreadful extravagance, says, "Whattaya crazy? Should never have married ya. Biggest mistake of my life!''—how do you react? Up to now, you have made the mistake of taking him seriously. You have gone into the bathroom and wept. You would never think of reacting to your five-year-old this way. When he sticks his tongue out at you and says, "You don't love me!'' how do you react? Take him seriously? Go into the bathroom and weep? Of course not! "Please get out of the kitchen; Mommie's trying to get supper." Now ask yourself, what's the difference between a five-year-old and a thirty-five-year-old who is acting like a five-year-old? Treat him as you would your five-year-old. Not openly, of course, but in your mind's eye see him dressed like a five-year-old, complete with lollipop. That will get things in proper perspective in no time flat!

If People Insist On Acting Like Five-Year-Olds, Treat Them Like Five-Year-Olds

WORRY, WORRY!

Do you remember the old gag, "What do they do in Argentina when it rains?"—"They let it rain!" Precisely. That's what they do everyplace else. As Mark Twain said of the weather, "Everybody talks about it, but nobody does anything about it." You don't feel vaguely guilty because it's raining out instead of sunny. But you do worry and fret and mope and get frustrated about a good many things that you are no more able to control than you are the weather. Unless you are a very specially situated person, there is very little you can do about the international situation, inflation, strikes, modern education, government spending, current styles, etc. Worrying about things that you can do nothing about is a pretty silly way of making yourself miserable. Don't take the worries of the world on your shoulders.

DISASTER!

I'll never forget the time in February of 1962 when all the astrologers in India predicted the end of the world because of a severely malevolent conjunction of planets. I got a call from one of my more scatterbrained friends and she breathlessly asked, "Is the world going to come to an end next Tuesday or is it next Wednesday?" I answered, "Next Tuesday!" She rejoined, "Oh dear, oh dear, oh dear, what'll we do?" I said, "Don't worry, *that's just for India!*" She said, "Oh thank you so much! You can't *imagine* how *relieved* I am! You're a living doll!" I'm about as close to being a living doll as the Indian astrologers were to being prophets.

That's Only for India!

ATLAS

What can you do about the problems of our century? Well, you could run away from life and become a hermit. Pack up your bedding, bid farewell to newspapers, magazines, radio and TV and seek out a cave in a warm climate. Then "let the rest of the world go by." Or you can go to the other extreme and play Atlas. Atlas was a legendary figure, a north-African giant who held the universe on his shoulders. He is long gone, but he has many descendants. If you feel that you must take the problems of the world on your skinny shoulders, you are a little Atlas. You are one of those who feel that you are morally obligated to become involved with any problem situation that comes to your attention. Let's say that you are watching TV and you see that there is a revolution in Patagonia. Immediately you feel obligated to do something about Patagonia. If there is nothing you can do (as is usually the case), you don't let it go at that. No, you must worry about it. "Poor Patagonia! I must find something to do about it, or I just won't sleep tonight!"

Don't Try To Carry The World On Your Shoulders You're No Atlas

THE REALIST

You don't have to be a hermit or a Little
Atlas. There is a middle ground. Be a realist;
be reasonable. Keep informed as to what is
going on in your neighborhood, your town,
your state, your country and the world in
general. If there is anything in any of these
areas that you can do to right a wrong, correct
an error, fill a material or spiritual need, do
it! Father Keller of the Christophers has the
slogan, "It is better to light one candle than to
curse the darkness." If there is nothing that
you can do about a worrisome situation, either
by personal action or through channels, put it
out of your mind. Force yourself not to think
about it. Forget it, at least until such time as
you can do something about it. Ask God to
take care of it. Operate on the principle—the
realistic principle—that whatever is beyond
your control is not your concern. Then you can
divert all the psychic energy you have been
wasting on ineffectual fretting into some

productive, useful channel. And you'll feel much better, in the bargain.

Anything Beyond Your Control Is Not Your Problem

THE MANAGERIAL SYNDROME

There are three main types of the Little Atlas personality—the global, the community, and the family Little Atlas. All share in what well might be called the Managerial Syndrome. The syndrome consists of a hefty endowment of self-importance, officiousness, wisdom, omnicompetence and an unbounded capacity for meddling, taking care of situations and giving unwanted advice, or, in a word, conceit.

Although it is generally futile to try and figure out why anyone does anything, nevertheless it is fascinating to speculate on why some people are always trying to manage other people, either individually or in the mass. Basically, the managerial or reforming instinct, the "let me counsel you from the height of my superior wisdom" phenomenon seems to be innate in human nature. We love to tell others what to do. We are all tempted, at times, to try to control or at least to influence the beliefs, attitudes and actions of others. And depending on circumstances, we all seem to be able to find good and sufficient reasons for our meddling. But actually, nothing justifies it; it is immoral.

AUTONOMY

The Creator has endowed every human being with the right to live his own life. With this God-given right goes responsibility for one's actions. Without freedom there can be no responsibility. Because of my freedom of choice, I must accept responsibility for my actions. You have no right to coerce me into a course of action that I reject, regardless of whether my course of action is morally right or wrong. You are responsible for your actions; you are not responsible for mine, and I am not responsible for yours. Even God does not interfere with or violate this autonomy. When He created man, He created him with the power to do wrong. He warned man that doing wrong would cause him unhappiness, but nevertheless, He never deprived man of freedom to choose to do wrong. He never used His almighty power to prevent man from exercising this freedom of choice. Nor has He delegated to any of His creatures the right to enforce righteousness by physical force or intimidation. God respects your neighbor's right to freedom of thought and action; do you?

Keep Your Own Nose Clean. Let Others Worry About Theirs

AUTHORITY

What we have said about autonomy is true in the private sphere. There is a factor, however, which to some extent modifies one's autonomy: that is the common good, the good of the group. Every group must have rules, and must have sanctions to enforce them, and someone with the authority to impose the sanctions. This is true in the family, in the government, in the military service, in education, and to some extent in business and industry. Every type of society rests on the principle of authority as its foundation. The parent, the teacher, the elected official, the magistrate, the policeman, the military officer, the business executive—all possess and exercise legitimate authority. But the limits of this authority are well defined, and it is only within these limits that one having authority may direct or dictate the actions of others.

If you have authority, you have a duty to those who are subject to you. You have the obligation of making known to your subjects, in clear and unmistakable terms, what is required of them: of rewarding or applying sanctions to them according to their performance. Beyond that, any attempt to force acquiescence is an invasion of an individual's rights. If you are the parent, for instance, of a five-year-old, you can and should dictate his behavior; but it's rather ridiculous to maintain that the same holds true in regard to a thirty- or forty-year-old son or daughter, married or single.

Don't Try To Exceed Your Authority

THE GLOBAL LITTLE ATLAS

Before we get into a discussion of the Managerial Syndrome at the family level, it might be well to consider the syndrome on the neighborhood and worldwide level. To be a Global Little Atlas, you must know everything about everything and have the solution to every problem. You can play this role in a fairly harmless way by aspiring to be the armchair Global Atlas type. All that is necessary is that you assume a profound air, speak slowly and portentously, pat your paunch, puff your pipe, and pontificate to all who will listen on the World Situation. You might even write a syndicated column and make a fortune.

The Professional Global Little Atlas is a horse of a different color. He is first and foremost an Intellectual, generally an author, quite often a sociologist or psychologist, and generally gets his start in a university. He is then gradually introduced into the government as a consultant and quite often winds up in a position of power, either as the director of a mammoth private foundation, or in the halls of the Legislature, even in the President's Cabinet itself. His aim in life is to manipulate people in the mass toward his favorite social-ist-centralist-welfare-state goal. He operates, he would have you believe, from plain and simple altruism—the betterment of society. He may even have convinced himself of this. But scratch the skin of this humanitarian, and you will find underneath the power-hungry idea-logue. He is just dying to manipulate millions and millions of people here and abroad, by every means from compulsory birth-control to compulsory fluoridation. He will rescue us poor slobs from our slough of despond whether we want to be rescued or not. It's only for our own good! After all, social progress has its price, as witness the Ukrainian Kulaks of the twenties, or the contemporary workers in the Siberian salt mines of the sixties. The Global Little Atlas is hard at work, with Messianic zeal, striving to bring about the Millenium on earth. If the innate dignity of the human being, based on his freedom, goes down the drain in the process (as it must), it's all right; the poor slob really didn't know how to use it, anyway!

SMALL-TOWN LITTLE ATLAS

Ever hear of Carrie Nation? She was a little old lady who broke up saloons with a hatchet. She was opposed to drinking. She was bound and determined to liberate the poor slaves of Demon Rum if it took a hatchet to do it. Needless to say, she failed, because it takes more than a hatchet to do it. Even the Eighteenth Amendment couldn't do it. Because no one can liberate a slave who loves his chains. Well, anyway, Carrie has more than her share of spiritual descendents. They are variously known as reformers, buttinskis, busybodies, or do-gooders. If you are of the Small-Town-Little-Atlases, you feel that you have the burden of seeing to it that all your friends, acquaintances, neighbors and relatives live right. Quite a task, getting everyone to think right and live right (that is, to live in the way you think is right and act in the way you think is right). Let's say you have given up smoking. Fine! Bully for you. But that means that you must rescue everyone you can from the subtle, physical, moral, and emotional perils of this noxious addiction. So you go about snatching brands from the burning, advising, counseling, warning, correcting, helping—whether the objects of your misplaced solicitude want to be advised, counseled, warned, corrected and helped, or not. Be warned that your well meant efforts are in vain; not only that, they will boomerang. The longer you stick at your vain endeavor, the more you are going to add to the strain and tension of attempting the impossible. Frustration will be your lot. Perhaps a breakdown, if you work hard enough at it! If you would be delivered from this fate, learn and take to heart, this very minute, the Eleventh Commandment: MIND YOUR OWN BUSINESS!

A key problem to the person afflicted with the Managerial Syndrome is the matter of determining where his own business leaves off and other people's begin. Do you have this problem? Or do you know the difference, and make other people's business your business anyway? If so, shame on you! Know the realist's rule, and accept it: What is beyond your control is not your concern! What is not your concern is none of your business. Don't make it your business!

Mind Your Own Business

THE FANATIC

There is a special breed of Small Town Atlas known as the fanatic. He is not content just to ride the hobby horse to death; oh, no, he must convert everyone else to his own extreme way of thinking. If people wish to go to extremes without bothering anyone else, more power to them. But they have no right to try and bully all their relatives and friends into going along with them. There are various types of fanatics: the religious nut, the diet nut, the nutrition nut, the vitamin nut, the teetotaler, the fresh air nut, the golf nut, the nicotine nut, and what have you. It would seem to me that these people are uncertain of their own convictions and are seeking to reinforce them by inflicting them on others. They are the antithesis of "Live and Let Live." Now, how about you?

THE FAMILY LITTLE ATLAS

Parents have a difficult role to play in the Live and Let Live way of life. They are responsible for their children, until their children reach maturity. They have the obligation of bringing up their children. This means that they must teach them by word and example what is to be expected of them. They must lay down rules and enforce them with sanctions. In a way, they most certainly are living their children's lives for them. No one can fill this role perfectly. There are many pitfalls to be avoided. If you are the parent of young children and are not fairly stable emotionally, you will probably fall into one of the three most common ones: possessiveness, vicarious ambition, and the popularity contest. Any one of these can pervert the parental role and harm the emotional growth of the child. All are indications of an emotional imbalance in the parent, taken out on the child.

MAMA

First we have the possessive mother. Suffice to say that her many rationalizations—"I just live for my son!''—are fairly transparent, adding insult to injury by putting the veneer of maternal solicitude over pride, vanity, emptiness and the desire for power. Some highly respected observers believe that one of the fundamental causes of the degeneration of our culture is the Mama's Boy. Enough said!

DEAR OLD DAD

Then there is the ambitious father. He feels deeply his own failure to measure up to his own standards of achievement, so he is going to achieve through "the boy." "The boy" is going to college, even though he wants to be a mechanic. "The boy" is going to be a star in the Little League, even though he is all thumbs. And so forth. What a prescription for frustration and misery! Needless to say, in the long run, the ambitious parent merely lays up for himself resentment and frustration. If you are trying to make over your child into an ideal image of what you believe yourself to be or what you should have been, stop it right this minute!

At the other end of the scale, we have the father who wants to be a pal. Not only does he let his kids live, he lets them do what they please. He thinks family life is a popularity contest. In his immaturity, being insecure as to his own ability to evoke love in his children, he tries to bribe them. Never disciplines them, and interferes when his desperate wife tries to. Woos them with gifts and money. Kids in this situation have to have an unusually strong natural emotional endowment to grow up to be solid citizens.

MY BROTHER'S KEEPER?

If you have an adult relative whose behavior is scandalous, you are being severely tempted to live his (or her) life for him. Most people succumb to this temptation because they feel that it is their duty. Indeed, most of your friends and relatives believe the same thing. It is a universal myth, and should be squashed once and for all. Supposing you are the wife or mother of a middleaged alcoholic, and you are using every device under the sun to "make him stop drinking." Someone asks you why are you doing this. You consider this a silly question: "Because he's my son (or husband), of course." Your answer includes two false presuppositions: first, that there is some way in which you can make him stop drinking; and secondly, that it is your obligation to make him stop drinking. You may as well face the truth; even if he begs you to help him stop drinking, there is nothing that you can do that will help him stop drinking. That is something that he must do himself. He can get help, but you are not the person to give it. You can best help him by telling him this. If he wants to know who can help him, tell him: Alcoholics Anonymous. If his problem is not drinking but some emotional problem, the same holds true: he must apply to a competent person, namely a psychiatrist. You do not qualify.

Everyone seems to think that you are responsible for the behavior of your husband or wife, or of your grown son or daughter. In other words, that it is your obligation as the parent or spouse to get the wayward person to shape up. It's, so to speak, part of your job. Well, is it? Hardly! You are responsible to yourself and to God for yourself and for no other adult human being, regardless of blood relationship. You cannot take the blame for what any other adult does, and you cannot put on any other human being the responsibility for what you do, regardless of what relationship he may have to you. That is the basis of the whole "Live and Let Live" philosophy.

You Are Responsible
For Yourself
To God and To Yourself.
You Are Not Responsible
For Any Other
Adult Human Being

BLACK SHEEP

Perhaps you are the parent of a grown-up son or daughter whose behavior is disgraceful—the black sheep of the family. You feel that you should "do something about it." Why? "Because he's disgracing the family." So you argue with him, cajole, bribe, threaten, or otherwise try to get him to change his behavior. Stop a minute and consider the fact that he is not disgracing the family. He is disgracing himself. The only one who can disgrace you is you. And you can't disgrace anyone else, or "let them down." The only one you can disgrace or let down is yourself. You are no more responsible for the behavior of a grown son or daughter, brother or sister, uncle or aunt than you would be responsible for the behavior of the man or woman down the street. Refusal to accept this fact can lead only to needless and wasted guilt and frustration.

No One Can Disgrace Anyone But Himself

"WHERE HAVE I FAILED?"

While we're on the subject, to just what extent is a parent responsible for the aberrant behavior of a grown-up child? Traditional psychology generally manages to blame everyone but the patient for his aberrations. Don't fall for it! In my opinion, the major determinant of a person's behavior is his native emotional and spiritual endowment. His temperament is inherited from a million ancestors. Which one will you point the finger at? His training in the family circle will influence him, it is true; but it is hardly the decisive factor in his eventual attitude and behavior. So the usual chant of "Son, where did we fail you?" seems a little silly. Don't assume responsibility for your black sheep, and, above all, stop trying to make him over into a white one!

OPEN SEASON ON SPOUSES

Marriage vows have been the putative source of many evils, real and fancied. One prominent clergyman has been known to remark that in certain instances he feels that in officiating at a marriage he is compounding a felony. There is no question but that a certain type of person regards the marriage vows as a license to regulate his or her spouse's life in every department. Some husbands believe their marriage contract empowers them to dictate to their wives in everything from the way they do their hair to the question of whether or not they shall "be allowed" to smoke or drive a car. But it works the other way round: many a wife believes that her "I do" is a commission from on high to make her mate over according to her private blueprint—a sort of second creation. This is one situation where everyone would be better off if "Love, Honor and Obey" read rather "Live and Let Live."

Accept Your Spouse
For Better Or For Worse
Especially for Worse

PART III

ME, MYSELF AND GOD

THE SUPREME BEING

Up to this point, we have been considering our relationship to ourselves—the real Myself and the Pseudo I (Buster or Brat, as the case may be)—as well as our relationship to others. Hereafter we will be concerned with our relationship to One who affects us in every way and in every relationship—our relationship to ourselves and our relationship to one another. Some people call Him the Higher Power; others, The Supreme Being; and still others, God.

This part of *Me, Myself And You* is addressed to those who believe in a higher power, or would like to believe. In other words, it is assumed that if you read on, you are willing to include faith in a Supreme Being in your scheme of things. Hence no time or effort will be expended in arguing His existence.

GOD LOVES ME!

On vacation recently I was picking up supplies at the general store when a rather wild-eyed Jesus Freak burst in on the scene and demanded: "Brother, how do you know God loves you?"—"Because I'm here!" I guess he had never gotten the right answer before, because it stopped him cold for a minute. He blurted out, "Amen, Brother!" and bolted out. It should be obvious that if a Supreme Being created me, He must love me personally. He could have created a million other people in place of me, but He chose to create me. He must have liked the idea of me—yes, me!—before He created the universe some 14 billion years ago, and here I am.

There is an old saying to the effect that there are some people that only a mother could love. That should be amended: God loves people that even their mothers can't love. And that's about as far as you can go. God loves me. Can I believe it? Why on earth not?

Lord I Believe
Help My Unbelief

OUR FATHER

God loves me as a father loves his child.
After all, He is my Father, the source of my
being. He is the perfect father; His love for me
is selfless. He is kind, understanding, indul-
gent—but strict when my good requires it. He
wants to see me do well. He wants to be able
to be proud of me, to be able to say, "That's
my boy" or, "What do you think of my little
girl?" He will do everything in His limitless
power to help me. Like any father, He wants
me to feel free to come to Him in difficulties.
Like every parent from time immemorial, He
grieves, in a sense, at the lack of communication between us. I may, like many a child,
have the feeling that my parent just wouldn't
understand—we're just not on the same wave-
length. Or too often I may react to Him as a
child does when he knows he's been naughty,
and have the urge to keep out of sight, to lie
low until it blows over or is forgotten.

"But I just can't face up to God! What
must He think of me? I don't dare even to try

to talk to Him anymore!'' Well, just what do you think He expects of you? Miracles? The important thing is that He expects you to *trust* Him, above all else. He expects you to love Him and to serve Him to the best of your knowledge and ability, but the main thing is that He expects you to believe in the fact that He loves you. Not only to believe that He loves you, but to act as if you believed it. Very few people have been able to love and serve God perfectly, and you are no exception. You are not expected to love and serve Him perfectly. As a matter of fact, by yourself you can't even begin to do it. But that isn't necessary: all that is required is that you have the *willingness* to do it, admit that it's beyond your powers, and ask Him to help you to do it. You must want to do it, and have enough faith in His love for you as to believe that He can and will enable you to do it. "Dear God, You know I am just a poor slob. Help me!''

Try Trusting God

POOR SLOB!

We have noted that the rigorous program of self-discipline which has been recommended as the solution to your emotional and living problems is a pretty large order. If you feel that it's beyond you, remember that help is available instantly, at all hours of the day and night. If you can't find the necessary courage and strength in yourself, He is ready and willing to provide it. You see, He wants you to become the person that He intended you to be—might even say hoped you to be—when He decided to create you. He wants this even more than you do. With His help, you can and will become that person.

"But when I pray, I don't really feel that there is anyone listening. It's like talking in a vacuum. I feel like an idiot." Okay! Feelings aren't facts. Because you feel it is so doesn't make it so. Go through the motions. Pray as if you really believed someone was listening. Do this for a month, and see what happens. After all, what have you got to lose?

Maybe you don't feel "worthy," whatever that is supposed to mean, all right, so you're not "worthy." Well, who is? What human being isn't a poor slob, at least from time to time? And there's no pecking order for poor slobs. The least you can do is to say every morning, "Dear God, I want to get through this day without giving in to (you name it): discouragement, inadequacy, self-doubt, anger, resentment, anxiety, self-pity, or whatever. But I can't, by myself; you can enable me to. Please do. I place myself in your hands, just for today." Then take a minute to thank Him at night for doing just that—because He will. As an old black friend of mine puts it: "Dear God, don't let anything happen to me today that the two of us can't handle."

Dear God, You Know I'm Just a Poor Slob Help Me!

DOES HE
REALLY UNDERSTAND ME?

Most of us have had the experience of getting into trouble and turning to a good friend for help. You know he won't condemn you, lecture you, or say "How stupid can you get!" You know he likes you not because of what you are, but despite what you are. His instantaneous reaction is "What can I do to help?" Now tell me, why is it that you take it for granted that another human being can understand your difficulties and will be eager to help, while at the same time you deny this confidence and trust to the One who is actually your best friend? Because, perhaps, you never think of Him as your best friend? Very few people do.

It may be that you are afraid to approach Him because you have offended Him. That's natural, but it's a mistake. Take yourself: are you so small that a friend in difficulties would be afraid to seek your help when you are the only one who can help him, just because he had displeased or even offended you in the past? I'm sure you would feel aggrieved that he thought so little of you and your friendship. So it must be with God. We mustn't make the mistake of judging Him by ourselves. He loves you with a love that knows no bounds—He *is* love. That love cannot be affected, altered, diminished, or destroyed by anything we prodigals may do. This means, in effect, that he does not stop loving us when we offend Him. Further, He keeps on loving us even while we persist in offending Him and refuse to repent. "To understand all is to forgive all." That, without doubt, is an exaggeration, but it certainly gets across the general idea. When are you going to swallow your pride and go to Him?

IT'S NO GOOD

"It's no good; try as hard as I can, I just can't do it." There are many things you want to do—that you feel you must do—for yourself and others; you have tried your best but failed. So you give up. Try again, but this time, don't do it all on your own; ask Him to help you. Let His strength make up for your weakness. As long as He is in the picture, you may be helpless, but surely not hopeless. You may have to do this on sheer faith at first, but it won't be long before you are doing it out of conviction, because somehow or other what you couldn't accomplish before by yourself is getting done. Perhaps not in the way you expected, but done, nevertheless. It may take a while for it to dawn on you that those "coincidences" are not coincidences at all. It's no accident! That's when faith gives way to conviction, and you're on the way.

You Do Your Best
Let God Do The Rest

SERMONETTE

God is all-loving; He wants what's best for you.

God is all-knowing; He knows what's best for you.

God is all-powerful; He can do what's best for you.

What are you waiting for?

HELP!

It's a commonplace that "no man is an island." We are all interdependent. The lone wolf generally starves to death. We need others, and they need us. We need God most of all. And He likes it that way. He just can't resist an appeal for help. (Which is natural; ask any woman about the "helpless act." Especially when she has a flat tire.) Do you need help with your problem—physical, mental, spiritual, or whatever? When the average person gets in beyond his depth, he generally looks up the best lawyer, doctor, or businessman he can get hold of. First, among his friends and associates, because that way he just might get the solution for free. Or then again, his friend the lawyer might say, "Why not hire a lawyer?" But it's worth a try. Well, why not go to God for help? After all, He is not only your friend, but your Father, and fathers don't generally charge their children for professional services rendered.

Go To The Top

GET IN TOUCH

Prayer is talking to God. It's difficult, because it's like a one-way phone conversation. But you know He's on the other end of the line. What do you talk to God about? Well, ordinary conversation with your friends and associates wouldn't win any Nobel prizes for literature or Critics' Drama Circle awards for dialogue. Mostly it's informal and consists of a discussion of the weather, your health, taxes, the high cost of living, etc. Pretty trivial, when played back. Then why do you think that when you talk to God you have to give orations, make speeches and recite at Him? True, you do discuss some mighty serious things; you acknowledge that He is the Creator, Ruler, and Conserver of all things, including you. That He is the Lord of all. That you are nothing without Him, and depend on Him for everything, even your heartbeat. You admit that by yourself you can't do much—life is so complicated, and you're no Superman. Then you proceed to ask Him for the help you need. You need it all down the line. You need spiritual help for such things as overcoming your pesky faults and increasing your faith in Him and love for Him and your fellowman. Living problems (i.e., people problems.) Mental and emotional hangups. Material things. You name it. You might even ask Him to help you change your way of living, if you finally come to realize that that is what is necessary to make you and others happy.

After you make your requests, don't just go out and sit under the apple tree and wait for them to be granted. Might be a long wait! Roll up your sleeves, make with the muscles, work at it. It's still true that God helps those who help themselves.

Give Us This Day. . . . . . .

A ONE-WAY STREET?

You must have a fairly good idea of what God expects of you in the way of behavior. Now you wouldn't think of imposing on your friends—at least, not beyond a certain point. So if you expect God's help, you must be fair with Him. No relationship can be a one-way street. It's just that if you're all "gimme" and no "give," you can't be very proud of yourself. So you owe it to yourself as well as to Him to do all in your power to do what you believe He expects of you. Granted that you may not be able to live up to what you believe He expects of you, even with His help, you must do your best. That's all he asks, really—He doesn't expect success, but He does expect effort. And rewards it.

AMENDS

Almost everyone has done something in his life that he has good reason to regret, even to be heartily ashamed of. He may even have wronged others seriously, and felt remorse for years afterward. "I wish I'd never done it; I'd give anything to undo it. I'd like to make amends, somehow, but it's impossible." No, it is not impossible. There is Someone to Whom nothing is impossible. Even turning back the clock, even bringing good out of evil. You can even go so far as to ask Him to make the person you wronged better off in the long run than he would have been if you had never had anything to do with him. And be confident that it will be so!

St. Augustine: "God can bring good out of evil; even out of sin; even out of *my* sin."

PARTNERSHIP

Tired of going it alone? Everybody else fail you? You have a Partner. A Silent Partner. Between the two of you, there is nothing you can't do. It may take a long time—much longer than you think it should. It probably won't come out the way you want it, but then, you never were much of a long-range planner, and your Partner is. You may have to suffer along the way, but in the end you'll be thankful that you had to. You may, indeed you must, accept His way of doing things rather than your own. But after all, your way of doing things is precisely what got you where you are, and you should be ready to hand it over to Someone Else for a change. Besides, He never fails.

Over To You, Lord!

WRAP-UP

Happiness and contentment do not just happen. You have to work for them. Achieving comfortable living is the work of a lifetime; it is one's true life work. The secret is simple enough: to live, that is, to learn to control the things that are subject to our control; and to let live, that is, to learn to accept the things that are beyond our control.

Other people's thoughts, attitudes and actions are beyond our control; we learn to refrain from trying to control them. Even if we could control them through physical or moral force, we have no right to do so. Any attempt to interfere with the lives of others results only in misery and frustration for everyone.

We must learn to live our own lives. We cannot afford to be swayed either by our own emotions or by the reactions of others. This requires self-discipline—the hardest thing in the world to practice, but the most rewarding. It is the ultimate source of peace and contentment. When we have reached the point where we are no longer subject to the dictates of our emotional self within or to the actual or anticipated reactions of others without, we have arrived. We can truly call our souls our own.

If this is too big an order for us, it can still be done. The necessary help is there and waiting. All we have to do is to believe firmly that it will be given us, and ASK for it. "Ask, and you shall receive . . . " This uncertain life affords no guarantees of happiness, but if there is one certain pathway to contentment, it is marked "LIVE AND LET LIVE." And to make assurance doubly sure, "LET GO AND LET GOD!"